The Quinquennial Report of Religious Institutes to the Holy See

A Historical Synopsis and a Commentary

This dissertation was approved by the Rev. Romaeus O'Brien, O. Carm., M.A., J.C.D., as director, and by the Right Rev. Clement V. Bastnagel, S.T.L., J.U.D., and the Rev. Meletius M. Wojnar, O.S.B.M., S.T.L., J.C.D., as readers.

THE CATHOLIC UNIVERSITY OF AMERICA
CANON LAW STUDIES
No. 422

The Quinquennial Report of Religious Institutes to the Holy See

A HISTORICAL SYNOPSIS AND A COMMENTARY

A DISSERTATION

Submitted to the Faculty of the School of Canon Law of the Catholic University of America in Partial Fulfillment of the Requirements for the Degree of Doctor of Canon Law

BY

Mel Lawrence Brady, O.F.M., B.A., J.C.L.
A Priest of the Province of Saint John the Baptist

THE CATHOLIC UNIVERSITY OF AMERICA PRESS
WASHINGTON, D. C.
1963

Nihil Obstat:

Roger Huser, O.F.M., J.C.D.
Luke Bertsch, O.F.M., J.C.D.
Censores Provinciae

Imprimi potest:

Sylvan Becker, O.F.M.
Minister Provincial

July 2, 1962

Nihil Obstat:

Romaeus O'Brien, O. Carm., J.C.D.
Censor Deputatus

Imprimatur:

✠ Patrick A. O'Boyle
Archbishop of Washington

May 26, 1962

Printed by

Typographia Collegii S. Bonaventurae

Ad Claras Aquas (Quaracchi, Italia)

AFFECTIONATELY DEDICATED

TO

MY MOTHER

AND TO

THE MEMORY OF MY FATHER

FOREWORD

Pope Pius XI, in his Apostolic Letter *Unigenitus Dei Filius*, expressed the mind of the Holy See regarding its solicitous supervision of the Church's religious institutes. "The Apostolic See," he wrote, "under whose banner the orders of religious serve, being mindful of the benefits which in the course of time they have conferred on God's Church and on the state, has always attended to them with a special care and favor. For, besides the fact that it has taken upon itself to review and approve their laws and statutes, and has throughout the adversities of various times and circumstances zealously defended their cause, it has, moreover, not neglected to call them back, when necessary, to the former dignity and holiness of the institute." [1]

This zeal for the preservation of the dignity and holiness of religious life has manifested itself in various ways through the course of the centuries. It is manifested in our day in the form of the quinquennial report prescribed by canon 510 of the Code of Canon Law [2] and regulated by the decree *Cum transactis.* [3] It is the purpose of the present work to study the provisions of this canon and of the decree, so that from a better understanding of them the good intended by the quinquennial report may be fostered and better achieved. Pope Pius XII has spoken about this specific goal:

1 19 mart. 1924 — *Acta Apostolicae Sedis, Commentarium Officiale* (Romae: Typis Polyglottis Vaticanis, 1909-), XVI (1924), 134 (hereafter cited *AAS*).

2 Can. 510: "Abbas Primas, Superior Congregationis monasticae et cuiusvis religionis iuris pontificii Moderator supremus debet quinto quoque anno vel saepius, si ita ferant constitutiones, relationem de statu religionis ad Sanctam Sedem per documentum mittere, subsignatum a se cum suo Consilio et, si agatur de Congregatione mulierum, etiam ab Ordinario loci in quo suprema Antistita cum suo Consilio residet." — *Codex Iuris Canonici Pii X Pontificis Maximi iussu digestus Benedicti Papae XV auctoritate promulgatus* (Romae: Typis Polyglottis Vaticanis, 1917). (Hereafter reference to this work is made merely by means of the abbreviation "can." for canon and "cc." for canons, followed by the appropriate number.)

3 S. Cong. de Rel., 9 iul. 1947 — *AAS*, XL (1948), 378-381.

What concerns the relations of the states of perfection to the Vicar of Christ and the Holy See scarcely needs to be recalled: the prerogatives of the Apostolic See which are based on their institution by Christ himself and which the Church in the course of the centuries has only clarified and defined more accurately, must remain inviolable and sacred. Whereas all the faithful respect and observe them, members of the states of perfection will in this regard be an example to all. It is important, then, to seek and maintain contact with the Holy See. In the Encyclical *Humani Generis*[4] We pointed out that the tendency to avoid contact and to keep away was one important reason for the errors and deviations which it exposed; and this regrettable attitude was particularly that of some members of states of perfection. If this contact is to be fruitful it must be full of confidence, sincerity and docility.

The Holy See would like to receive from you information which is not only truthful but frank, such as to present the actual state of each community as regards doctrine and way of living, ascetical training and observance, religious discipline, temporal administration, and so on. Only then will it be possible to promote what is good and correct what is wrong before it is too late; for it is in these favorable spiritual dispositions that the replies, regulations and instructions of the Holy See bear fruit.[5]

The quinquennial report required by canon 510 does not stand isolated, and, as it were, marking a new point of departure for the Holy See whereby it has suddenly busied itself with the affairs of religious. Rather, it is an outgrowth of many centuries of supervision on its part. Accordingly, Chapter I of this dissertation traces the development of this supervision from the dawn of the Christian

[4] 12 aug. 1950—*AAS*, XLII (1950), 561-578.

[5] Pius XII, allocutio, 9 dec. 1957—*AAS*, L (1958), 41-42; translation from Bouscaren-O'Connor, *The Canon Law Digest* (4 vols. and Supplement through 1960, Milwaukee: The Bruce Publishing Company, 1934-1961), Supplement, Canon 487, pp. 15-16 (hereafter cited *CLD*).

era to the IV Lateran Council, when complete authority over new institutes was assumed by the Holy See. In Chapter II, varied means of supervision are examined whereby the Holy See implemented its desires for supervision over religious institutes. Chapter III outlines the historical development of reports concerning religious as required by the Holy See. Such reports can be seen as the final step before the Code in the development of the supervision of religious by the Holy See.

Part II considers the quinquennial report as introduced by the Code of Canon Law and as applied in practice through subsequent decrees of the Sacred Congregation of Religious. Accordingly, Chapter IV details the requirements of the Code and of these decrees. The chapters following examine these requirements by way of canonical commentary. Thus Chapter V studies the report as an instrument of supervision of religious by the Holy See, while Chapter VI considers how the report may serve as a means of supervision by religious superiors. The function of the local ordinary in relation to the quinquennial report is the subject of Chapter VII. The final chapter, Chapter VIII, views the report as a source of doctrinal interpretation of some canons of the Code.

The writer welcomes this occasion to express his sincere gratitude to his Franciscan superiors, particularly the Very Reverend Fathers Romuald Mollaun, O.F.M., and Vincent Kroger, O.F.M., former Ministers Provincial, and the Very Reverend Sylvan Becker, O.F.M., present Minister Provincial, for the opportunity of advanced study in Canon Law at the Catholic University of America. The writer also wishes to thank the members of the Faculty of the School of Canon Law for their kind assistance, and especially the Reverend Romaeus O'Brien, O. Carm., the director of this dissertation. Finally the writer expresses his appreciation for the encouragement and assistance given him by his brother, Reverend Ignatius Brady, O.F.M., who saw the copy through the press, by the Reverend Dismas Bonner, O.F.M., and by the Very Reverend Elio Gambari, S.M.M., member of the Sacred Congregation of Religious.

TABLE OF CONTENTS

PART ONE

HISTORICAL SYNOPSIS

CHAPTER I

THE BEGINNINGS OF PAPAL SUPERVISION

ARTICLE I. THE FIRST CENTURIES OF RELIGIOUS LIFE

Christ's invitation to a life of perfection [1] was not without fruit from the earliest years of the Church. Although dedicated virgins, ascetics and confessors are found perhaps already in the first century [2] — certainly in the second [3] — it cannot be said that their status was that of true religious. Before the middle of the third century, when monachism first appeared, [4] they remained with their family. [5]

The rise of organized religious life centered about the great monastic leaders of the third century, St. Paul (228-341) and St. Anthony (251-356). They and their followers were monks in the original sense of the word, that is, solitaries or hermits. [6] St. Pachomius (292-346) is credited with introducing a new type of monasticism, the cenobitic life, wherein monks lived a common life in a monastery according to a written rule and under the direction of specified superiors. Indeed, St. Pachomius was unique in this that, already in the fourth century, he set up a centralized government with all the monasteries subordinated to a superior general. [7] St. Basil (329-379) perfected the institute of cenobitic

1 Cf. Matthew, 19: 16-21; Luke, 9: 57-62; 14: 26-27; 18: 18-30.

2 Creusen, *De Iuridica Status Religiosi Evolutione* (2. ed., Romae: Apud Aedes Pontificiae Universitatis Gregorianae, 1948), p. 12.

3 Cf. St. Justin, *Apologia Prima pro Christianis,* Cap. 15 — Migne, *Patrologiae Cursus Completus, Series Graeca* (161 vols., Parisiis, 1857-1866), VI, 350.

4 Tabera, "De Ordinatione Status Monachalis in Fontibus Iustinianeis," *Commentarium pro Religiosis* (Romae: 1920-1934; ab anno 1935: *Commentarium pro Religiosis et Missionariis*), XIV (1933), 90 (hereafter cited *CpR* or *CpRM*).

5 Creusen, *De Iuridica Status Religiosi Evolutione,* p. 12.

6 Tabera, "art. cit.," — *CpR,* XIV (1933), 93.

7 *Ibid.,* 93-94.

life by means of a rule which required a perfectly common life in every respect. [8]

In the fourth and fifth centuries, monasticism spread from the East to the West under the influence of St. Athanasius (295-373), St. Ambrose (340-397), St. Jerome (342-420), St. Augustine (354-430), and others. [9] As in the East, monasteries were founded apart from any permission of the local ordinary. [10] And the members of these religious communities were considered subjects of the bishop in the same way as the rest of the faithful. [11]

Instances of supervision by the Holy See during this period are scarce. The first papal decretal which refers to religious [12] came from Pope St. Siricius (384-398) in 385. In a letter to Bishop Himerius of Tarragona in Spain he directed the bishop to expel from their monasteries certain delinquent religious. He also expressed the wish that worthy monks become clerics and even priests. To this end he established rules regarding the character and age of the ordinands. [13] The second papal reference to religious of this early period is found in a letter of Pope St. Innocent I (401-417) to Bishop Victricius in the year 404. Innocent prescribed that

8 Wernz, *Ius Decretalium ad Usum Praelectionum in Scholis Textus Iuris Canonici, sive Iuris Decretalium*, Vol. III, pars 2 (2. ed., Romae, 1908), n. 603.

9 Creusen, *De Iuridica Status Religiosi Evolutione*, pp. 15-16.

10 Orth, *The Approbation of Religious Institutes*, The Catholic University of America Canon Law Studies, No. 71 (Washington, D.C.: The Catholic University of America, 1931), p. 10.

11 Cf. Van Espen, *Ius Ecclesiasticum Universum* (2. ed., 4 vols., Lovanii et Lugduni, 1778), Pars III, tit. XII, Cap. 1, n. 7 (Tom. II, 407); Farrell, *The Rights and Duties of the Local Ordinary regarding Congregations of Women Religious of Pontifical Approval*, The Catholic University of America Canon Law Studies, No. 128 (Washington, D. C.: The Catholic University of America Press, 1941), p. 13 (hereafter cited *The Rights of Local Ordinaries*).

12 Vermeersch, "Religious Life," *The Catholic Encyclopedia* (15 vols., New York, 1907-1912; Index Vol., 1914; Supplement, 1922), XII, 751.

13 Mansi, *Sacrorum Conciliorum Nova et Amplissima Collectio* (53 vols. in 59, Parisiis, Arnhem, Lipsiae, 1901-1927), III, 655-661 (hereafter cited Mansi); Jaffé, *Regesta Pontificum Romanorum ab condita Ecclesia ad annum post Christum natum MCXCVIII* (editionem secundam correctam et auctam auspiciis Gulielmi Wattenbach, curaverunt S. Loewenfeld, F. Kaltenbrunner, P. Ewald, 2 vols. in 1, Lipsiae, 1885-1888), n. 255 (hereafter cited Jaffé).

monks who became clerics were not allowed to marry, despite the plea that other clerics of the same order had been allowed to marry. [14]

Although Pope St. Leo I (440–461) desired that the Council of Chalcedon (451) treat only of doctrinal matters, [15] the Council nevertheless enacted twenty eight disciplinary canons, ten of which pertained to religious. [16] Canon 4 stated that sincere monks were to be held in honor. In view of the abuses of some who used the monastic state for selfish ends, however, special regulations had to be adopted. Accordingly, the Fathers of the Council decided that the bishop's permission was necessary to build a monastery. They ruled that monks were to be subject to the bishop and remain in their monasteries unless they were assigned by the bishop to some work outside the monastery. Finally, the bishop was directed to exercise supervision over monasteries. [17]

In March of the year 453 Pope St. Leo sent to the bishops who had attended the council a circular letter in which he confirmed those acts of the council that referred to Catholic dogma, but he did not confirm the disciplinary canons. [18] Most of the disciplinary canons, however, and, in particular, canon 4, did become accepted in the West through custom and particular legislation. [19] The

[14] Jaffé, n. 286; Migne, *Patrologiae Cursus Completus, Series Latina* (221 vols. Parisiis, 1844-1855), XX, 478, and 479 with note *b* (hereafter cited *MPL*).

[15] In a letter to Maximus, Patriarch of Antioch (449–455), June 11, 453, Pope Leo stated: "Si quid sane ab his fratribus, quos ad sanctam synodum vice mea misi, praeter id, quod ad causam fidei pertinebat, gestum esse perhibetur, nullius erit penitus firmitatis: quia ad hoc tantum ab apostolica sunt Sede directi, ut, excisis haeresibus, Catholicae essent fidei defensores." — Mansi, VI, 241; Jaffé, n. 495. Cf. also his letter to Anatolius, Patriarch of Constantinople (449–458), May 22, 452 — Mansi, VI, 202; Jaffé, n. 483.

[16] Canons 2, 3, 4, 6, 7, 8, 16, 18, 23, 24. For the texts, cf. Schwartz, *Acta Conciliorum Oecumenicorum* (*a concilio Ephesino a. 431 ad conc. Constantinopolitanum a. 879*), 11 vols. in 4°, Tom. II, *Concilium Universale Chalcedonense*, Vol. 2, pars 2, *Rerum Chalcedonensium Collectio Vaticana, Canones et Symbolum* (Berolini et Lipsiae: Walter de Gruyter and Co., 1936), pp. [146]-[152].

[17] Schwartz, *ibid.*, p. [147].

[18] Mansi, VI, 226–228.

[19] Creusen, *De Iuridica Status Religiosi Evolutione*, p. 18.

result was that the authority of bishops over monks and monasteries as expressed in the Council of Chalcedon was generally received and approved in the West.[20]

After the legislation of the Council of Chalcedon and its subsequent reception in the West, each monastery was in fact a diocesan institute.[21] Until the time of Pope St. Gregory the Great (590-604), there was no noteworthy papal legislation of a supervisory character for religious.

It was in this period between Chalcedon and Gregory that St. Benedict of Nursia (c. 480-c. 547) established the foundations which were to have such a profound effect upon monastic life and the life of the Church as well. Actually, his monastic foundations did not immediately involve a change in regard to papal supervision. In fact, he did not even obtain papal approbation of his rule, since such approbation was not required at the time.[22] But if St. Benedict himself was not involved in the advancement of papal supervision, the same was not true of his sons. The next few centuries present a picture that is a composite of many interrelated factors which conspired to effect a radical change in the jurisprudence governing religious life.

Article II. Pope St. Gregory I

Pope St. Gregory was the first pope to legislate extensively for religious. Much of his legislation was directed to the protection of monastic rights. He desired to set a middle course which would offer mutual safeguards to the rights of monks and bishops. Antipathies between the two groups had been building up gradually, with the monks tending toward excessive independence, while bishops strove to extend their authority beyond that given them by law.

[20] Van Espen, *Ius Ecclesiasticum Universum*, Pars III, tit. XII, cap. 1, nn. 14-19 (II, 407, 408).

[21] Reilly, *The Visitation of Religious*, The Catholic University of America Canon Law Studies, No. 112 (Washington, D. C.. The Catholic University of America, 1938), p. 33.

[22] Orth, *The Approbation of Religious Institutes*, p. 21.

Gregory's provisions for the proper liberty of monks can be classified under three headings: (1) provisions pertaining to monastic freedom in the election of the abbot; (2) provisions pertaining to the rights of the monks in their free administration of the goods of the monastery; and (3) provisions in favor of cloistral observance, which restricted the bishop from celebrating public Masses in the churches of the monasteries. [23]

Gregory's efforts were also directed to the supervision of internal affairs of monastic life. While he encouraged the founding of monasteries, he did not neglect to correct lapsed discipline in older monasteries, and to direct reform when necessary. In fact, this latter purpose forms the theme of a majority of his decretals on religious. In repressing abuses, he sought the aid of the local bishop, the abbot, or both, to undertake an investigation or to mete out the appropriate punishment.

The abuses he strove to eliminate often touched on the fundamentals of monastic life, such as the non-observance of the vows of poverty and chastity, or the violation by wandering monks of the vow of conventual stability. He often corrected negligent abbots. Again, some of the irregularities he sought to correct were not so fundamental, but nevertheless they were abuses whose effects could work almost equal harm to religious discipline. Thus Gregory appointed secular procurators to take care of the external business affairs of nuns, so that their pursuit of perfection would be free from worldly contacts.

Not all of Gregory's decretals dealt with abuses. For example, he encouraged study in moderation. He set the age of sixty as the minimum age requirement for an abbess. He lengthened the period of novitiate to two years, and established rules for the admission of civil officials and soldiers into monasteries. Gregory favored the ordination of monks for the service of the monastery itself. But if an ordained monk wished to serve outside the monastery, he had to leave the monastery, after obtaining the permission of the

23 Fogliasso, *De Extensionis Iuridici Instituti Exemptionis Religiosorum* (Romae: Apud Custodiam Librariam Pont. Instituti Utriusque Iuris, 1948), pp. 90-91 (hereafter cited *De Extensione Exemptionis*).

abbot, and live as a secular priest. On the other hand, a secular priest who wished to become a monk had first to give up the care of souls in the world.[24]

Such legislation as Gregory enacted clearly points to a remarkably increased supervision of religious by the Holy See. As a result of his efforts, monasticism was very definitely brought into a closer relationship with the Holy See.[25]

Article III. The first exemptions

Through the extension of the privilege of exemption to many institutes a closer supervision of religious by the Holy See was fostered. The first exemptions were granted to Irish monasteries founded on the continent. St. Columban (543-615) claimed for his houses in Gaul, Switzerland and Italy the same rights his monasteries had enjoyed in Ireland,[26] where the abbot exercised jurisdiction over the monks, secular priests, and even the bishop.[27] On the continent this claim for the monks led to disputes between the local bishops and the Irish monastic foundations. Abbot Bartulphus of Bobbio, Italy, petitioned Pope Honorius I (625-638) for a solution of the problem. Honorius replied in the year 628 by granting the first full privilege of exemption. According to this privilege, he placed the monastery under the authority of the abbot and prohibited any secular ordinary lower than the pope from exercising authority in the monastery.[28] Two monasteries in Benevento received similar grants in 714 and 741.[29]

Closer papal supervision of religious was even more notable in the exemptions granted by the Holy See to combat lay proprietorship of monasteries and lay investiture. In post-Carolingian

[24] This summary is based on Dudden, *Gregory the Great* (2 vols., London, 1905) II, 173-185; 190-192.

[25] Dudden, *ibid.*, p. 173.

[26] Kurtscheid, *Historia Iuris Canonici*, Vol. I, *Historia Institutorum* (Romae: Officium Libri Catholici, 1941), p. 360 (hereafter cited *Historia Institutorum*).

[27] Fogliasso, *De Extensione Exemptionis*, p. 94.

[28] Jaffé, n. 2017; *MPL*, 80, 483-484; cf. Fogliasso, *op. cit.*, p. 96.

[29] Fogliasso, *loc. cit.*

times most monasteries were subjected to private ownership in one way or another as personal possessions or through feudal commendation.[30] Accordingly, the independence of monasteries as religious institutes was practically non-existent. Abbots and abbesses were instituted by the owner. The proprietor had the right to the income of the monastery. Some proprietors even arrogated to themselves the right to prescribe the particular rule by which monks or nuns should live.[31] The evils of the proprietary system were heightened by the practice of lay investiture, which became prevalent with the growth of feudalism.[32]

With a view towards protecting monasteries from the abuses inherent in private ownership, the popes began to take monasteries under their protection. With reference to the monasteries of the Frankish kingdom alone, there were 49 such indults granted in the years 855 to 900.[33] In the ninth, early tenth, and eleventh centuries,[34] the papacy increasingly assumed proprietary rights over monasteries and groups of monasteries. The Roman Curia phrased its grants in such a way that a proprietary relationship, as it were, arose between itself and the monasteries, whereby they were prevented from falling back into private ownership. At the same time, this relationship effectively precluded a recurrence of interference on the part of kings, bishops or others. In petitioning for this relationship with the Holy See, the monasteries, for their part, desired only the protection of the Holy See against the evils men-

30 Knowles, *The Monastic Order in England* (Cambridge: The University Press, 1941), p. 569.

31 Kurtscheid, *Historia Institutorum*, p. 275.

32 "In the tenth century the practice grew up of clothing the conferment of bishoprics and abbeys in the form of enfeoffment, and carrying it out in a solemn act which was known, from the end of the next century, as investiture." — Stutz, "The Proprietary Church as an Element of Mediaeval Germanic Ecclesiastical Law," in *Mediaeval Germany, 911-1250: Essays by German Historians*, trans. by Barraclough, 2 vols. (Oxford: Basil Blackwell, Ltd., 1938), Vol. II, 41-44 (hereafter cited *Mediaeval Germany*).

33 Kurtscheid, *Historia Institutorum*, p. 308 and n. 2.

34 Because of the "eclipse of papal prestige in the tenth century, the protection of St. Peter counted for little." — Knowles, *The Monastic Order in England*, p. 571.

tioned. They did not seek, however, a relationship with the Holy See which would be identified with the one to be discarded. In this they were not disappointed. The subsequent relations between the Holy See and the monasteries give no evidence of the domination hitherto exercised by private owners. In contrast with the former proprietors, the papacy did not interfere in the material or spiritual government of the monastery; nor did it usurp the income of the house. Papal ownership, therefore, was a benevolent one which operated for the increased freedom of the monasteries rather than for a temporal domination over them.[35] The monasteries, in turn, strove for a perfection of religious observance which would measure up to the ways approved for them by the Holy See.

A notable section of this body of papal monasteries consisted of the new monastic congregations which played an important role in the reform program. Thus, there were the monasteries of Cluny, of the Vallumbrosans, and of the Camaldolese. Before the rise of these congregations of monasteries, papal protection had been granted only to individual monasteries. But these new and vigorous monastic foundations were recognized by the Holy See as a potent force for reform in the restoration of monastic independence, and also a strong ally in striving after the crushing of lay investiture. Cluny, which had been founded in 910 as a monastery free from secular control, was organized into a monastic congregation and placed under papal protection in 1097 by Pope Urban II (1088-1099).[36] The Vallumbrosans received a similar grant from the same Pope in 1090,[37] while the Camaldolese achieved this status under Pope Paschal II (1099-1118) in 1113.[38]

As a result of this prodigious growth of monasteries and monastic congregations in direct subordination to the direction of

[35] Cf. Hirsch, "The Constitutional History of the Reformed Monasteries during the Investiture Contest," in *Mediaeval Germany*, pp. 135-145; Knowles, *ibid.*, pp. 570-571.

[36] Cf. Fogliasso, *De Extensione Exemptionis*, pp. 97-98.

[37] *MPL*, CLI, 322-324.

[38] Jaffé, n. 6357; *MPL*, CLXIII, 330-332.

the Holy See, papal supervision of religious and their way of life was quite extensive by the end of the eleventh century. In addition to the fact that the papacy had a comprehensive knowledge of almost all existing monastic bodies, [39] it was able to direct them through the relationship established by privilege, and by enactment of pertinent laws. [40]

[39] Knowles, *The Monastic Order in England*, p. 572.

[40] Creusen, *De Iuridica Status Religiosi Evolutione*, p. 25.

CHAPTER II

METHODS OF PONTIFICAL SUPERVISION

ARTICLE I. APPROBATION OF RELIGIOUS INSTITUTES

Section 1. Religious Orders

From the Council of Chalcedon until the IV Lateran Council (1215) there was no change in the law that the approval of the bishop was necessary for the founding of a monastery. At the latter Council, however, Pope Innocent III (1198-1216) decreed that no one should found a new religious order. [1] The Pope desired to forestall confusion in the Church, caused by too great a multiplicity of religious institutes. This papal prohibition against the erection of new orders in effect reserved to the Holy See the approval of any new religious institute, and thus placed every new institute under the scrutiny of the Holy See.

Repeating this prescription, the II Council of Lyons (1274) abolished all orders founded since 1215 without the approval of the Holy See. Mendicant orders which had been approved after the IV Lateran Council were foredoomed to a slow death, inasmuch as the profession of new members or the acquisition of new houses was forbidden. The canon expressly stated, however, that it did not extend to the Order of Preachers, the Order of Friars

[1] Can. 13: "Ne nimis religionum diversitas gravem in Ecclesia Dei confusionem inducat, firmiter prohibemus ne quis de cetero novam religionem inveniat; sed quicumque voluerit ad religionem converti, unam de approbatis assumat. Similiter qui voluerit religiosam domum fundare de novo, regulam et institutionem accipiat de religionibus approbatis."—Mansi, XXII, 1002; Schroeder, *Disciplinary Decrees of the General Councils*, Text, translation and commentary (St. Louis, Mo.: B. Herder Co., 1937), pp. 254-255 (hereafter cited *Disciplinary Decrees*).

Minor, the Order of Carmel, or the Hermits of St. Augustine. The latter two were *pro tempore* allowed to continue. [2]

The Franciscans had been orally approved by Innocent III himself in 1209. [3] Honorius III (1216-1227) solemnly approved the order on November 29, 1223. [4] The Dominicans had been approved by Honorius III in 1216, [5] and the Carmelites were approved by the same Pope in 1226. [6] The Hermits of St. Augustine, united in one institute, received approbation from Alexander IV (1254-1261) in 1256. [7]

Section 2. Religious Congregations

Despite the legislation of the IV Lateran Council and of the II Council of Lyons, communities of members who professed only simple vows arose in the Church. Commentators have advanced two theories in an attempt to explain why these congregations were founded in seeming contradiction to the general law. One explanation holds that, with the tacit approval of the Holy See, a contrary custom became established which allowed local ordinaries to approve new institutes without obtaining pontifical approval. [8]

[2] Can. 23 — Mansi, XXIV, 96-97; Schroeder, *Disciplinary Decrees*, p. 351. This prescription was included in the *Liber Sextus*, in c. un., *de religiosis domibus*, III, 17, with this difference that Boniface VIII removed all doubt about the status of the Carmelites and the Augustinians by changing the clause which had simply conceded their temporary continuance. The decretal employed the words "*in solido statu volumus permanere.*"

[3] Holzapfel, *Manuale Historiae Ordinis Fratrum Minorum*, latine redditum a G. Hasselbeck (Friburgi Brisgoviae, 1909), p. 5.

[4] Bulla, *Solet annuere — Bullarium Franciscanum Romanorum Pontificum*, ed. Ioannes Sbaralea (Vol. I-IV, Romae, 1759-1768); ed. Conradus Eubel (Vol. V-VII, Romae, 1898-1904), I, 15-19 (hereafter cited *Bull. Franc.*).

[5] Bulla, *Religiosam — Bullarium Ordinis Fratrum Praedicatorum*, ed. a Ripoll, recognitum a Bremond (8 vols., Romae, 1729-1740), I, 2-3.

[6] Bulla, *Ut vivendi — Bullarium Diplomatum et Privilegiorum Sanctorum Romanorum Pontificum Taurinensis Editio* (24 vols. et Appendix, Augustae Taurinorum et Neapoli, 1857-1872), III, 415 (hereafter cited *Bull. Rom.*).

[7] Bulla, *Licet — Bull. Rom.*, III, 635-636.

[8] Bouix, *Tractatus de Iure Regularium* (3. ed., 2 vols., Parisiis, 1882-1883) I, 210.

The second theory is that, since institutes of simple vows did not exist at the time of the IV Lateran Council, the legislator had no intention of prohibiting their foundation. [9] In view of the comprehensive wording of the legislation of Innocent III, which prohibited any religious institute to be founded in the future, it seems that the law extended also to congregations of simple vows. Therefore, the explanation based on the existence of a contrary custom offers a more reasonable explanation. [10]

The fact remains that such congregations did arise at an increased rate in the centuries following the IV Lateran Council. Pope Leo X (1513-1521) acknowledged the existence of some tertiary communities, praised the good works done by them, and even wrote a special rule for them. This rule was to become a model for many religious communities of women. [11] Pope St. Pius V (1566-1572), however, soon issued legislation which required that all women religious take solemn vows and observe the cloister. [12] Thus, in effect, he removed the legal status of congregations of simple vows. Nevertheless, they continued to grow in number; and documents favorable to them, but falling short of full and explicit approval, were issued by Clement IX (1667-1669), [13] Clement XI (1700-1721), [14] and Benedict XIV (1740-1758). The latter pope explicitly allowed the formation of a congregation of simple

[9] Cf. Toso, *Ad Codicem Iuris Canonici Commentaria Minora* (5 vols., Romae: Marietti, 1920-1927), lib. II, pars II, p. 14; Chelodi, *Ius de Personis iuxta Codicem Iuris Canonici, Praemisso Tractatu de Principiis et Fontibus Iuris Canonici* (ed. altera, a Sac. Ernesto Bertagnolli recognita et aucta, Tridenti: Libr. Edit. Tridentum, 1927), p. 411, footnote 1.

[10] Cf. Quinn, *Relation of the Local Ordinary to Religious of Diocesan Approval*, Catholic University of America Canon Law Studies, No. 283 (Washington, D.C.: The Catholic University of America Press, 1949), pp. 27-28.

[11] Leo X, const. *Inter cetera*, 20 ian. 1521 — *Bull. Rom.*, V, 764-767. Cf. Freriks, *Religious Congregations in their External Relations*, The Catholic University of America Canon Law Studies, No. 1 (Washington, D. C., 1916), pp. 14, 19.

[12] Const. *Circa pastoralis*, 29 maii 1566 — *Bull. Rom.*, VII, 447-450.

[13] Const. *Alias propositas*, 10 dec. 1667 — *Bull. Rom.*, XVII, 609-610.

[14] Const. *Inscrutabili*, 13 iun. 1703 — as discussed and quoted by Muzzarelli, *De Congregationibus Iuris Dioecesani* (Romae: Apud Piam Societatem a S. Paulo Apostolo, 1943), pp. 20-21.

vows under the supervision of the local ordinary; there was, however, no positive approval of the institute by the Holy See.[15] Although Benedict XIV's constitution concerned only one particular case, it was truly a milestone in the evolution of congregations of simple vows.[16] For it set a practical precedent, being "so clear in setting forth the rights of ordinaries in relation to these communities that it became the established guide and norm for all religious congregations until the year 1900. Rome did not refuse from that time on to approve and confirm the rules of new religious congregations."[17] In the nineteenth century it became the policy of the Holy See to include in the approbation of rules and constitutions an approbation of the institute itself.[18]

This policy of the Holy See finally crystallized in the constitution of Leo XIII (1878-1903), *Conditae a Christo.* In this important document the Pope defined the juridical character of institutes both of diocesan and pontifical approval, as well as the function of the local ordinary in their supervision.[19]

A supplement to *Conditae a Christo*, the *Normae*, was promulgated by the Sacred Congregation of Bishops and Regulars in 1901.[20] Even though these *Normae*, published as guides to be followed in the formation of institutes, were not laws, they embodied the official *stylus curiae*, and bishops were to observe them if

15 Const. *Quamvis iusto*, 30 apr. 1749— *Codicis Iuris Canonici Fontes*, cura E.mi Petri Card. Gasparri editi (9 vols., Romae [postea Civitate Vaticana]: Typis Polyglottis Vaticanis, 1923-1939; Vols. VII-IX, ed. cura et studio E.mi Iustiniani Card. Serédi) n. 398 (hereafter cited *Fontes*).

16 Larraona, "Commentarium Codicis," *CpR*, I (1920), 133.

17 Orth, *The Approbation of Religious Institutes*, p. 57.

18 Larraona, "Commentarium Codicis," — *CpR*, I (1920), 133; cf. Bizzarri, *Collectanea in usum Secretariae S. C. Episcoporum et Regularium* (2. ed., Romae, 1885), pp. 808-814, for a list of such approbations in the nineteenth century; *ibid.*, pp. 772-773, for the method followed by the S. Cong. of Bishops and Regulars in approving institutes of simple vows (hereafter cited *Collectanea*).

19 Leo XIII, const. *Conditae a Christo*, 8 dec. 1900 — *Fontes*, n. 644.

20 *Normae Secundum quas S. Congr. Episcoporum et Regularium Procedere Solet in Approbandis Novis Institutis Votorum Simplicium* (Romae: 1901) (hereafter cited *Normae*).

institutes founded by themselves were later to obtain pontifical approval. [21]

It can be seen, then, that in the area of the approbation of religious institutes the supervisory enactments of the Holy See became increasingly detailed and effective during the period immediately preceding the promulgation of the Code of Canon Law.

Article II. Supervisory Agents of the Holy See

Over and beyond a general supervision effected by the requirement of papal approbation for an institute, the Holy See supervised particular areas of discipline through agents acting on its authority.

Section 1. Cardinal Protectors

One of these agents was the cardinal protector. St. Francis of Assisi is credited with introducing into religious life the functions of a cardinal protector. [22] In his rule Francis commanded superiors of the order to ask the pope for a cardinal to be the director, protector and corrector of the fraternity. [23] Following this example, other orders obtained cardinal protectors.

Before the complete development of the Roman Curia and its congregations, the position of the cardinal protector was an important one, especially for conducting negotiations between the Holy See and religious orders. [24] In many cases he exercised jurisdiction over the religious order. [25] Thus, for example, Urban IV (1261-1264) placed the Poor Clares under their protector rather

21 Orth, *The Approbation of Religious Institutes*, pp. 70-71.

22 Larraona, "Commentarium Codicis," — *CpR*, VI (1925), 127.

23 *Regula S. Francisci*, Cap. XII: " Ad haec per obedientiam iniungo ministris, ut petant a Domino Papa unum de sanctae Romanae Ecclesiae cardinalibus, qui sit gubernator, protector et corrector istius fraternitatis; ut semper subditi et subiecti pedibus eiusdem sanctae Ecclesiae, ... quod firmiter promisimus, observemus." — *Regula et Constitutiones Generales Ordinis Fratrum Minorum* (Romae: Curia Generalis Ordinis, 1953), p. xii.

24 Larraona, "Commentarium Codicis," — *CpR*, VI (1925), 128, and note 31.

25 Bouix, *Tractatus de Jure Regularium*, II, 167-168.

than under the superiors of the Order of Friars Minor.[26] Similarly, Sixtus IV (1471-1484) conferred extensive authority on the cardinal protector of the Carmelites.[27]

Gradually, in many orders, the authority of the cardinal protector became so extensive that he exercised jurisdiction over individual provinces, convents, and even over individual religious, countermanding the orders of legitimate superiors. Thus, an office which had begun as an agency of the Holy See for the supervision of religious became at times a source of abuse, and a danger to religious discipline.[28] Taking cognizance of these harmful developments, Pope Innocent XII (1691-1700) reduced the power of the cardinal protector, so that he no longer exercised authority over the institute or its members in virtue of his office.[29]

Section 2. Supervisors of the Cloister

Pope Boniface VIII (1294-1303) introduced the first general law imposing a strict cloister on nuns.[30] Not only were regular superiors ordered to enforce its observance, but he also commanded local ordinaries to enforce this prescription. The authority upon which the latter were to base their directives is of special significance. If the convents were subject to local ordinaries, they were to act on their own authority; but if they were immediately subject to the Holy See, the ordinaries were to act in virtue of the authority of the Holy See. That this latter provision involved a special delegation from the pope is seen from Boniface's statement that the bishop did not thereby acquire jurisdiction over the nuns in other matters.[31]

26 Bulla, *Beata Clara*, 18 oct. 1263, Cap. XXV — *Bull. Franc.*, II, 520.

27 Bouix, *loc. cit.*

28 Cf. Bernardino da Siena, *Il Cardinale Protettore negli Istituti Religiosi specialmente negli Ordini Francescani*, Dissertatio ad Lauream in Facultate Iuris Canonici Pontificiae Universitatis Gregorianae (Firenze: Industria Tipografica Fiorentina, 1940), pp. 77-104.

29 Const. *Christifidelium*, 16 febr. 1694 — *Fontes*, n. 257.

30 Schaaf, *The Cloister*, The Catholic University of America Canon Law Studies No. 13 (Cincinnati, Ohio, 1921), p. 43.

31 Cf. c. un., *de statu regularium*, III, 16, in VI°.

The Council of Trent likewise directed the local ordinary to enforce the strict enclosure of nuns. This he was to do on his own authority in monasteries subject to him, and by the authority of the Apostolic See in exempt monasteries.[32]

Pope St. Pius V provided that nuns who violated the cloister were to be compelled by local ordinaries, in cooperation with the regular superiors, to observe it. The power of local ordinaries in regard to the cloister was further specified by the prescription that they and the regular superiors were not to allow more nuns to be admitted than monasteries could support with their usual alms. Local ordinaries were to promulgate these provisions and they were authorized to enforce them with their own authority, or with the authority of the Holy See when a monastery was exempt.[33] Thus St. Pius V continued the Tridentine policy of papal supervision and control, even over exempt nuns, through the agency of the local ordinary.

Clement VIII (1592-1605) reiterated a prescription of the Council of Trent,[34] when he directed superiors to heed the admonition of the local ordinary and to punish regulars living within the monastery whenever they were guilty of scandalous crimes committed outside the cloister. Superiors were forbidden, under severe penalties, to transfer a delinquent religious to another diocese without punishing him. In the event that they did this, and furthermore refused to recall the religious for punishment, the ordinary of the diocese to which the religious had been sent was delegated by the Holy See to punish the delinquent.[35]

Section 3. Visitators of Religious

Another medium employed by the Holy See for supervision can be discerned in the first universal legislation regarding the

32 Conc. Trident., sess. XXV, *de regularibus*, c. 5 — Schroeder, *Canons and Decrees of the Council of Trent* (St. Louis: B. Herder Book Co., 1941), pp. 220-221 (hereafter cited *The Council of Trent*).

33 Pius V, const. *Circa pastoralis*, 29 maii 1566 — *Bull. Rom.*, VII, 447-450.

34 Conc. Trident., sess. XXV, *de regularibus*, c. 14 — Schroeder, *The Council of Trent*, p. 226.

35 Clement VIII, const. *Suscepti muneris*, 23 febr. 1596 — *Fontes*, n. 181.

visitation of religious. Pope Innocent III required that religious orders hold a chapter in each province every three years. At these chapters prudent religious were to be appointed for the purpose of canonically visiting the monasteries in the province. The significant point in this prescription is the fact that these visitators functioned in the name of the pope rather than in the name of the chapter. [36]

A similar arrangement was employed by Pope Clement V. He required the local bishop to conduct the visitation of the monasteries of nuns. If the nuns were exempt, the visitation was conducted in virtue of the authority of the Holy See, and the bishop was to enforce religious observance even in exempt monasteries. [37]

The Council of Trent likewise appointed local ordinaries to be the agents of the Holy See in the supervision of religious. Exempt monasteries of the same or neighboring ecclesiastical provinces were supposed to form a congregation. Chapters were to meet every three years, and the superiors elected therein were to work for reform and were to enforce the sacred canons and the decrees of the Council of Trent. For this purpose the superiors, as well as the visitators elected by the chapter, were to make visitations frequently. Relative to these visitations, there were two instances in which local ordinaries were to act with authority delegated from the Holy See. First, if the monasteries failed to meet in chapter to form the prescribed congregations, the metropolitan was directed to convoke the chapter. Secondly, if the superiors and visitors failed in their duty even though they had been warned by the metropolitan, they were to be subject to the bishop of the place as a delegate of the Holy See. [38]

36 C. 7, X, *de statu monachorum et canonicorum regularium*, III, 35.

37 C. 2, *de statu monachorum vel canonicorum regularium*, III, 10, in Clem.

38 Conc. Trident., sess. XXV, *de regularibus*, c. 8 — Schroeder, *The Council of Trent*, pp. 222-223. It can be concluded from the general wording of the decree that the local ordinary was not merely to exercise the authority of a canonical visitor. Rather, if the religious failed to comply with the prescriptions of the decree, they were to be subject to the bishop as to a superior, acting with general authority delegated by the Holy See: "Quod si etiam metropolitano instante praedicta exequi non curaverint, episcopis, in quorum dioecesibus loca praedicta sita sunt, tanquam sedis apostolicae delegatis subdantur".

If regular observance was not maintained in independent monasteries, then the abuse was to be corrected through visitations by local ordinaries acting as delegates of the Holy See.[39] In other instances, too, the bishop was empowered to institute a canonical visitation of religious. Thus, for example, a bishop could proceed as a visitor against a regular living outside his monastery, whenever he was guilty of a crime or serious delinquency. In such circumstances he was not exempt from the visitation, punishment and correction of the local ordinary, who was to act as a delegate of the Holy See.[40]

Monasteries of exempt nuns were to be supervised by the bishop acting upon the authority of the Apostolic See. This supervision included the right and the duty of visitation.[41]

Later legislation also constituted local ordinaries as delegates of the Holy See in the visitation and correction of religious. In 1625 Urban VIII, through the Sacred Congregation of the Council, decreed that all religious houses which contained less than twelve members were subject to the visitation, correction and complete jurisdiction of the local ordinary.[42] Innocent X (1644-1655) ordered that a number of small monasteries be suppressed, since he regarded them as a detriment to religious discipline.[43] Some of these monasteries were exempted from this suppression, while others that had been suppressed were soon restored.[44] The same Pope decreed the following for these small convents: (1) until the revived convents consisted of twelve members, they were subjected to the visitation, correction and jurisdiction of the local ordinary; (2) if the monasteries which had been exempted from suppression did not have at least six members, they were subject to the bishop in the same manner. In both these cases the bish-

[39] Conc. Trident., sess. XXI, *de ref.*, c. 8 — Schroeder, *ibid.*, p. 141.

[40] Conc. Trident., sess. VI, *de ref.*, c. 3 — Schroeder, *ibid.*, p. 49.

[41] Conc. Trident., sess. XXV, *de regularibus*, c. 9; sess. VII, *de ref.*, cc. 7, 8; sess. XXIV, *de ref.*, c. 10 — Schroeder, *ibid.*, pp. 223, 58, 199.

[42] S.C.C., decr. 21 iun. 1625, § 14 — *Fontes*, n. 2460.

[43] Const. *Instaurandae*, 15 oct. 1652 — *Fontes*, n. 233.

[44] Reilly, *The Visitation of Religious*, pp. 68-69.

op was to exercise his jurisdiction as a delegate of the Holy See.[45]

Section 4. The Roman Curia

With the reorganization of the Roman Curia in the latter half of the sixteenth century, the supervision of religious was facilitated for the Holy See by means of special agencies constituted for that purpose.

Shortly after the close of the Council of Trent, Pope Pius IV (1559-1565) instituted in the Roman Curia the Congregation of the Council.[46] It had been the intention of Pius IV that the Congregation aid him, personally, in interpreting the legislation of the Council of Trent. But from the time of Pope St. Pius V the Congregation was also given the ordinary power to interpret and to execute the Tridentine decrees.[47] In so far as these decrees touched upon religious, the Congregation of the Council had jurisdiction over regulars. By 1586, however, there was instituted by Pope Sixtus V a special congregation to supervise the religious life, the Congregation for the Consultation of Regulars.[48] The same Pope defined the competence of this Congregation. It had the faculty of interpreting the law by replying to doubts proposed by any religious order. It was to settle controversies which arose between orders, provided that in their settlement there was not required a form of judicial procedure. It could give permission for religious to transfer to another order. The cardinals of this Congregation were to hear and decide cases of apostates and fugitives. To the cardinals was committed also the execution of the mandates of apostolic visitors and of apostolic constitutions for religious. They were to choose zealous and learned regulars to act

45 Const. *Ut in parvis*, 10 febr. 1654—*Bull. Rom.*, XV, 754-755.

46 Motu propr. *Alias nos nonnullas*, 2 aug. 1564—Schroeder, *The Council of Trent*, pp. 538-539.

47 Monin. *De Curia Romana* (Lovanii, 1912), pp. 37-38.

48 Breve *Romanus Pontifex*, 17 maii 1586—*Analecta Iuris Pontificii*, Première Série (1855), col. 1371-1373.

as apostolic visitors. The cardinals of the Congregation were also to strive to promote and preserve harmony between subjects and superiors.[49]

In 1601 the Congregation for the Consultation of Regulars was joined to the Congregation of Bishops and other Prelates. The newly merged Congregation was called the Congregation of Bishops and Regulars.[50] As far as the supervision of religious was concerned, the scope of its competence remained the same. This Congregation operated *more principis*, summarily, and without much formality, after having simply inspected the truth of a situation. It often terminated controversies even through the use of secret information, employing the rules of prudence rather than strict legal formalities.[51]

The Congregation of Bishops and Regulars continued in existence and operation until the reorganization of the Roman Curia by Pope St. Pius X in 1908. It was not, however, the only Congregation which supervised the affairs of religious. In 1652 Innocent X (1644-1655) issued a constitution at least confirming, if not creating, the *Congregatio super statu Regularium*.[52] The function of this Congregation was to supervise the religious institutes of Italy.[53] This Congregation was abolished by Innocent XII (1691-1700) in 1698, and its faculties were given, partly to the Congregation of Bishops and Regulars, and partly to a new Congregation he had established, the *Congregatio super disciplina regulari*.[54]

The latter Congregation was to carry out the reforms of the Council of Trent and of the supreme pontiffs among all the reli-

49 Sixtus V, bulla *Immensa*, 22 ian. 1588, Congr. XI—*Bull. Rom.*, VIII, 993-994.

50 Monin, *De Curia Romana*, pp. 53-54.

51 Ferraris, *Bibliotheca Canonica, Iuridica, Moralis, Theologica, necnon Ascetica, Polemica, Rubristica, Historica* (9 vols., Romae, 1885-1889), s.v. *Congregationes Ecclesiasticae Romanae*, nn. 42, 43.

52 Const. *Instaurandae*, 15 oct. 1652—*Bull. Rom.*, XV, 696-700. Monin (1881-1954) held that the Congregation came into being some time during the three-year period preceding the constitution.—Monin, *De Curia Romana*, p. 60.

53 Clemens IX, const. *Iniuncti nobis*, 11 apr. 1668—*Bull. Rom.*, XVII, 654-657.

54 Bulla *Debitum*, 4 aug. 1698—*Bull. Rom.*, XX, 826.

gious in Italy. Therefore this Congregation had practically the same function as its predecessor. But it was given the added faculty to suggest to the Roman pontiff measures it judged necessary or useful for fostering regular observance in any religious institute of men wherever it was situated, even outside of Italy.[55] This Congregation was suppressed by Pope St. Pius X in 1906, and matters within its competence were given over to the direction of the Congregation of Bishops and Regulars.[56]

At the same time Pius X abolished another Congregation, one that had been created by Pius IX (1846-1878) in 1846, the *S. Congregatio de statu regularium ordinum.*[57] Pius IX had defined the purpose of this Congregation in two encyclical letters of the same date, the one sent to regular superiors and the other to bishops. Its task was to devise better means for restoring religious discipline, and to effect such a reform through its decrees.[58]

There were also two other Congregations which supervised religious in particular territories. The *Congregatio pro negotiis ecclesiasticis extraordinariis* attended to the affairs of religious in Russia and South America. And the *S. Congregatio de Propaganda Fide* supplied for the other curial agencies in mission territories and in the Oriental Churches.[59]

St. Pius X, who had already done some rearranging of the Curia in its task of supervising religious, effected further changes in this field in the curial reform of 1908. In his constitution *Sapienti consilio* he established the *S. Congregatio negotiis religiosorum sodalium praeposita,* commonly called the Sacred Congregation of Religious. It was to have within its jurisdiction all religious of simple and solemn vows, and the members of societies without vows, as well as the members of third orders secular. Any question which concerned these classes, whether it was among themselves,

55 *Loc. cit.*

56 Motu propr. *Sacrae Congregationi*, 26 maii 1906 — *Acta Sanctae Sedis* (41 vols., Romae, 1865-1908), XXXIX (1906), 203-204.

57 Pius X, *loc. cit.;* Bouix, *De Curia Romana* (2. ed., Parisiis, 1880), p. 191.

58 Litt. encycl. *Ubi primum* et *Cum hisce litteris*, 17 iun. 1847 — Bizzarri, *Collectanea*, pp. 815, 816.

59 Freriks, *Religious Congregations in their External Relations*, p. 80.

or between them and outsiders, even bishops, fell under the supervision of this Congregation. It was also to act as a tribunal in disciplinary cases concerning religious, except for cases reserved to the Holy Office; and it had the right to handle dispensations from the common law. [60]

The Congregation for the Propagation of the Faith was given jurisdiction over religious only in respect to their role of missionaries; and the Congregation for Extraordinary Ecclesiastical Affairs was not assigned any direct competence over religious. [61]

60 Const. *Sapienti consilio*, 29 iun. 1908 — *AAS*, I (1909), 11-12.

61 *Ibid.*, 12-14.

CHAPTER III

PRE-CODE REPORTS TO THE HOLY SEE

The Holy See persistently pursued a policy of supervision over religious in the centuries after the IV Lateran Council through the different agencies delineated in the preceding chapter. During this period there was gradually being formulated another method of supervision whereby the Holy See sought detailed information concerning religious institutes in the form of reports from local ordinaries and from the institutes themselves. Since the reports required by canon 510 and the subsequent decrees of the Holy See are the direct legal descendants of these reports, the present chapter will be devoted to this agency of supervision, which has been described as "the principal method employed by the Holy See to insure prudent administration and legislation for religious institutes." [1]

Article I. Reports from Local Ordinaries

Sixtus V, in 1585, [2] decreed that patriarchs, primates, archbishops and bishops should make a report to the Holy See at regular intervals of time, to be determined by their distance from Rome. The ordinary was to give an account of his pastoral office, and of all things pertaining to the care of souls entrusted to him. [3] The Pope did not specify in detail what was to be included in this general report. But Fagnani (1598-1678) composed a list of topics for the benefit of his contemporaries. He taught that the general

[1] Freriks, *Religious Congregations in their External Relations*, p. 82.

[2] For a concise synopsis of the history of this subject before the time of Sixtus V, cf. Benedictus XIV, *De Synodo Dioecesana* (2 vols., Parmae, 1764), Lib. XIII, cap. VI, n. 13.

[3] Sixtus V, const. *Romanus Pontifex*, 20 dec. 1585 — *Fontes*, n. 156.

norm of Sixtus V called for a report regarding the monasteries of men and women, especially with reference to their location, buildings, temporal goods, revenues, sacred furnishings and personnel. It was also to be reported whether the cloister of nuns was properly observed, and whether the nuns maintained the common life. [4]

An official formula for this report was issued in 1725 by the Sacred Congregation of the Council, at the request of Pope Benedict XIII (1724-1730). [5] The questionnaire was drawn up by the secretary of the Congregation, Prosper Lambertini (later to become Pope Benedict XIV), who testified that it was approved by Benedict XIII, and that it was endowed with public authority. [6] Accordingly, the Congregation of the Council required its use as a general rule. [7]

The formulary directed local ordinaries to report the number of monasteries of men and women existing in the places of their jurisdiction, with an indication as to which of these monasteries were subject to them. [8] In this report they were to give complete and detailed information on all aspects of the religious life of regulars in the diocese. [9] In regard to nuns subject to the local ordinary, he was to report on their fidelity to the constitutions; on the observance of the cloister; on possible abuses in their monasteries;

[4] Fagnanus, *Commentaria in Quinque Libros Decretalium* (4 vols., Venetiis, 1697). Lib. II, tit. 24, *de iureiurando*, cap. IV, nn. 73, 79.

[5] For the text, cf. *Acta et Decreta Sacrorum Conciliorum Recentiorum, Collectio Lacensis* (7 vols., Friburgi Brisgoviae, 1870-1892), I, 423-427 (hereafter cited *Coll. Lac.*).

[6] Benedictus XIV, *De Synodo Dioecesana*, Lib. XIII, cap. VI, n. 10. Some doubt was cast on the universal binding force of this formula, in view of the statement that Benedict XIII *very probably* extended its use to the whole Church. — Cf. Lucidi, *De Visitatione Sacrorum Liminum* (3. ed., 3 vols., ed. J. Schneider, Romae, 1883), I, 33. The Instruction itself, however, left no doubt that the use of the questionnaire was obligatory: "Haec idcirco Instructio publici iuris fit, ut in Relationibus statuum suarum Ecclesiarum, ad eandem Sac. Congregationem in posterum transmittendis, curent Episcopi, Archiepiscopi, Primates et Patriarchae ipsi se conformare." — *Coll. Lac.*, I, 423-424.

[7] Lucidi, *De Visitatione Sacrorum Liminum*, I, 33.

[8] S.C.C., instr., 1725, § I, n. VIII — *Coll. Lac.*, I, 424.

[9] *Ibid.*, § IV — *Coll. Lac.*, I, 425.

on the appointment of ordinary and extraordinary confessors; and on the financial administration of the monasteries of nuns. For monasteries of nuns subject to regulars, the bishop was to report on the observance of the cloister; on the approbation of confessors; and on the financial account concerning the nuns which was to be submitted through the regular superiors. [10]

Benedict XIV renewed Sixtus V's legislation, and extended to abbots and prelates *nullius* the obligation of making the report. [11]

More particular in scope was the report required from bishops before the Holy See would approve institutes of simple vows. Information was to be supplied regarding the purpose and scope of the institute, its beginning, the number of members and houses, the means of support. In addition, the petition was to demonstrate the utility to the Church of the institute, and also report upon the general progress of the society. [12]

In 1861 the Sacred Congregation for the Propagation of the Faith issued a formula to be used in the report submitted by local ordinaries of mission territories. There were fifteen questions concerning religious working in the missions. The ordinaries were to state the kind and number of religious present; how many religious houses there were; what was the state of their regular observance; how far they depended on the local ordinary; what their means of support was; and, finally, to what extent their help was an asset for the work of the missions. [13] A later formula published by this Congregation in 1877 did not demand such detailed information. Though some points about the regular observance were included, most of the questions pertained to the religious in their role as missionaries. [14]

The last formula for the report of the local ordinaries published before the Code came in 1909 from the Sacred Consistorial Congre-

[10] *Ibid.*, § V — *Coll. Lac.*, I, 426.

[11] Const. *Quod sancta*, 23 nov. 1740 — *Fontes*, n. 303.

[12] This report was not required by law, but by the *stylus* of the S. C. Ep. et Reg., as summarized by its secretary, Bishop Bizzarri (1802-1877), in Appendix I of his *Collectanea*, pp. 772-773.

[13] S.C. de Prop. Fide, litt. encycl., 24 apr. 1861, § II, nn. 36-50 — *Fontes*, n. 4853.

[14] S.C. de Prop. Fide, instr. (ad Vic. et Praef. Ap.), 1 iun. 1877 — *Fontes*, n. 4891.

gation, in conjunction with a decree which reorganized the matter of the *ad limina* visit of the bishops. [15] Appended to the decree was a new questionnaire. Chapter IX of this questionnaire concerned itself with institutes of men religious. The bishop was to report regarding their observance of the common life, their manner of dress, their means of support, and their reputation in the diocese. He was also to report whether any dismissed religious were in the diocese, and, if so, what sort of life they led. The ordinary was to specify what type of work the religious did, and whether the local ordinary himself supervised these works according to the norms of the law. Another point was the observance of the decrees of the Holy See by religious who were engaged in gathering alms. Additional information was required regarding the status of the relationship between the bishop and religious. Finally, he was to report whether there were any diocesan institutes of men, and, if so, whether their works contributed to the general good of the Church. [16]

In regard to women religious the ordinary was to report whether they were a source of good example. If there were nuns who were subject to regulars, the bishop was to note whether everything proceeded according to law. As for other institutes of women not subject to regulars he was to report on the observance of the cloister; on the administration of temporal goods and the investment of dowries; on the observance of papal decrees governing confessors; on the works of those given to the active life, especially concerning precautions taken by religious doing home nursing, or laboring in hospitals for men. If there were women religious engaged in gathering alms, there was to be a report on their observance of the decrees of the Holy See. Finally, the local ordinary was to report on the status of diocesan institutes of women in his diocese. [17]

[15] S. C. Consist., decr. *A remotissima,* 31 dec. 1909—*Fontes,* n. 2064.

[16] S. C. Consist., *Ordo servandus in relatione de statu ecclesiarum,* 31 dec. 1909, Cap. IX, nn. 102-106—*Fontes,* n. 2065.

[17] S. C. Consist., *ibid.,* Cap. X, nn. 107-113. A new formula published November 4, 1918, did not substantially alter the questions relating to religious, but served

ARTICLE II. REPORTS FROM RELIGIOUS SUPERIORS

Prior to the Code of Canon Law there was no general legislation requiring religious institutes to report to the Holy See regarding their spiritual and temporal status. From the time of the Council of Trent, reports were required in particular instances of certain institutes. These reports, in large measure occasional, served the Holy See in its task of enforcing the reform decrees. Thus, in 1599 Clement VIII instructed the superior general of the Order of Servites to present to his general chapter a report on the temporal affairs of the order and an account of his own administration. A copy of this report was to be retained for the Holy See in the event it was requested. [18]

In order to determine whether the religious houses of Italy had sufficient revenues to support their members, Paul V (1605-1621) asked for a report upon the movable and immovable property of these houses. [19]

A decree of the Sacred Congregation of the Council required religious superiors in Italy to submit to their general or provincial chapters an account of the revenues of each house. The chapter was to decide how many religious could then reside in each house, in proportion to its capacity of supporting them. A report of these proceedings was then to be sent to the Sacred Congregation within a year. [20] This decree was later renewed by Pope Innocent XII. [21]

---

to accommodate them to the new Code of Canon Law.—*AAS*, X (1918), 499-500. The same is to be said of the questionnaire issued by the Sacred Congregation for the Propagation of the Faith, April 16, 1922—*AAS*, XIV (1922), 293-294.

[18] Clement VIII, decr. *Nullus omnino*, 25 iul. 1599, § 6—*Bull. Rom.*, X, 664. This was not a general decree, since it was directed to the Servites, as noted by Gasparri in *Fontes*, n. 187, note 1, and by the editor of the *Bull. Rom.*, X, 662. The latter dates this decree March 20, 1601.

[19] Paul V, const. *Sanctissimus*, 4 dec. 1605—*Bull. Rom.*, XI, 249-250.

[20] S. C. C., decr. 21 iun. 1625, §§ 10, 11, 12—*Fontes*, n. 2460. Note that § 14 of this decree, which forbade houses of less than twelve members to be founded—or, if they were founded, subjected them to the jurisdiction of the local ordinary—applied universally. But the paragraphs requiring the reports applied only to Italy.

[21] Const. *Nuper*, 23 dec. 1697—*Fontes*, n. 260.

With the same purpose of apportioning the number of religious in each house according to the ability of the house to support them, Innocent X (1644-1655) had required a somewhat more detailed report from the convents of Italy. This report went further in that the history of the house, the exact location, the limit which had been placed on the number of members, and the names of all the religious and domestics actually residing there were to be given.[22]

In 1848 the *S. Congregatio super statu regularium* issued a lengthy decree for the houses of Italy on the reception of novices. The superiors were instructed to inform the Congregation every six months regarding the age, nationality, and qualities of each novice received. They were also to list the documents drawn up for the reception. Finally, they were to report about the observance of the decree in regard to the training of novices.[23]

In 1862 Pope Pius IX (1846-1878) decreed that the Franciscans should elect their Minister General for a twelve-year term, thus prolonging the term by six years. But at the end of the first six-year period there was to be held a general congregation of the provincial superiors; on that occasion the Minister General was to give a report of his administration, of the regular discipline, studies, the instruction of novices, and other matters pertaining to the order. The congregation itself was then to transmit this report to the Sacred Congregation of Bishops and Regulars. A similar decree was issued to the Dominicans and to the Capuchins.[24]

In its *animadversiones* on the constitutions approved for institutes of simple vows, the Sacred Congregation of Bishops and Regulars often required a periodic report on the state of the institute. Thus in 1860 the Congregation directed that the Congregation of the Resurrectionists send a biennial report about the state of the society.[25] In 1861 the obligation of making a triennial report

[22] Const. *Inter cetera*, 17 dec. 1649 — *Bull. Rom.*, XV, 646-649.

[23] Decr. *Regulari disciplinae*, 25 ian. 1848, Pars prima, art. XIV — Bizzarri, *Collectanea*, p. 837.

[24] S. C. Ep. et Reg., decr. 23 maii 1862 — Bizzarri, *Collectanea*, p. 154.

[25] S. C. Ep. et Reg., decr. 14 sept. 1860 — Bizzarri, *Collectanea*, p. 150.

was imposed on the Hospital Sisters of St. Paul. This report was to cover the state of the institute in regard to members, religious observance, the novitiate, and the general administration.[26] In the same year the Sisters of Nazareth of the dioecese of Chalons were instructed to make a report every three years. The information to be supplied included mention of the number of sisters and the number of houses; an evaluation of the observance of the constitutions; and an account of the financial administration.[27]

Actually, from 1861 onward, the practice of requiring a triennial report to the Holy See became a common procedure in the approbation of new institutes.[28] Such a report was not mentioned in Leo XIII's *Conditae a Christo*, but the *Normae* of 1901 directed that a triennial report, signed by the. local ordinary of the motherhouse, be sent to the Sacred Congregation of Bishops and Regulars.[29] Therefore, all new religious institutes were to insert such a provision in their constitutions if they expected pontifical approval. It will be noted, however, that the *Normae* did not affect existing pontifical institutes, although some of these on their own accord began the practice of sending reports.[30]

According to the *Normae*, the report was to cover the status of the institute in regard to personnel, temporal possessions, and discipline.[31] What the *Normae* lacked by way of further delineation was supplied by the canonical authors of the time. Bastien (1866-1940), for example, gave more detailed recommendations on what points were to be covered.[32] It was not long, however, before the Sacred Congregation of Bishops and Regulars published a comprehensive list of questions to be answered by those who were

26 S. C. Ep. et Reg., *Animadversiones*, 12 iul. 1861, n. 10—Bizzarri, *op. cit.*, p. 793.

27 S. C. Ep. et Reg., *Animadversiones*, 27 sept. 1861, n. 6—Bizzarri, *op. cit.*, p. 794.

28 Larraona, "Commentarium Codicis,"—*CpR*, VIII (1927), 275.

29 *Normae*, n. 262.

30 Larraona, *ibid.*, p. 276, note 430.

31 "Quovis triennio Moderatrix Generalis de statu sui Instituti disciplinari, materiali, personali et oeconomico ad S. Congregationem referat."—*Normae*, n. 262.

32 Bastien, *Directoire Canonique à l'Usage des Congrégations à Vœux Simples* (Abbaye de Maredsous, 1904), pp. 288-289.

obliged to make the report. The questionnaire contained 98 questions, arranged under three headings: persons, goods, and religious discipline. In addition to the questions covering these matters, there were also preliminary questions of a general nature regarding the date of pontifical approval of the institute, its purpose or scope, the number of members received in the past, and the time of the latest report to the Holy See. [33]

The information supplied by such questionnaires was indeed extensive. But the Sacred Congregation desired the answers in order to perfect the supervision of religious by the Holy See. [34]

[33] S. C. Ep. et Reg., decr. *In approbandis,* 16 iul. 1906—*Fontes,* n. 2052.

[34] "Huiusmodi enim relatione singula Instituta, quorum domus in variis extant dioecesibus dissitisque locis. explorata perspectaque fiunt eidem S. Sedi; quae idcirco continua providentia ea prosequi, et, si quando a legibus deflectere videantur, sive cohortationibus sive correctionibus mandatisque ad pristinam observationem revocare potest."—*Loc. cit.*

PART TWO

CANONICAL COMMENTARY

CHAPTER IV

POST-CODE REPORTS FROM RELIGIOUS

ARTICLE I. CANON 510

Canon 510 of the Code of Canon Law extended the obligation of making a periodic report to many religious institutes not previously bound to do so. According to this canon, the following are obliged to make a report: the abbot primate; the superior of a monastic congregation; and the superior general of institutes of pontifical right.[1] Accordingly, the superiors of independent monasteries were excused from the obligation of making this report. Likewise, the general superiors of institutes of diocesan approval were not bound to submit a report to the Holy See. However, in virtue of canon 675, superiors general of pontifically approved societies of the common life were bound to send the report.[2]

According to canon 510, the report was to be made every five years. However, if the constitutions of the institute were approved after the promulgation of the Code[3] and directed that the report be sent within a shorter period of time, the constitutions were to be followed. The canon further directed that the report be signed by the superior and by his council. In addition, the reports of congregations of women were to be signed by the local

[1] Can. 510: "Abbas Primas, Superior Congregationis monasticae et cuiusvis religionis iuris pontificii Moderator supremus debet quinto quoque anno vel saepius, si ita ferant constitutiones, relationem de statu religionis ad Sanctam Sedem per documentum mittere, subsignatum a se cum suo Consilio et, si agatur de Congregatione mulierum, etiam ab Ordinario loci in quo suprema Antistita cum suo Consilio residet."

[2] Can. 675: "Regimen determinatur in uniuscuiusque societatis constitutionibus; sed in omnibus serventur, congrua congruis referendo, can. 499-530."

[3] S. Cong. de Rel., decr. *Sancitum est*, 2 mart. 1922—*AAS*, XIV (1922), 161-163; tr. in *CLD* I, 282-283.

ordinary of the mother house. In the years immediately following the Code, there was no new questionnaire to be used in the compiling of the report. The report, therefore, was to follow the outline of the one published in 1906 by the Sacred Congregation of Bishops and Regulars. [4]

Article II. The Decree *Sancitum est*

In 1922 the Sacred Congregation of Religious in its decree *Sancitum est* further defined the obligation of making the report as prescribed in canon 510. [5] The canon required the report every five years. The decree fixed the five-year periods, beginning from January 1, 1923, according to the following pattern for the various religious institutes.

A. Communities of men:

1. In the first year of each five-year period (1923, 1928, 1933, etc.): canons regular, monks, military orders;
2. In the second year of each period (1924, 1929, 1934, etc.): the mendicant orders;
3. In the third year of each period (1925, 1930, 1935, etc.): clerics regular;
4. In the fourth year of each period (1926, 1931, 1936, etc.): clerical and lay congregations of simple vows;
5. In the fifth year of each period (1927, 1932, 1937, etc.): societies of the common life without public vows.

B. Communities of women:

The division was made according to the geographic location of the mother house of the institute, that is, the place where the superior general had her official residence. The allocation of the various years was as follows:

1. In the first year (1923, 1928, etc.): institutes in Italy, Spain and Portugal;
2. In the second year (1924, 1929, etc.): institutes in France, Belgium, Holland, England and Ireland;

[4] Cf. *supra*, p. 31 f.

[5] Cf. *AAS, loc. cit.*

3. In the third year (1925, 1930, etc.): institutes in the remaining regions of Europe;
4. In the fourth year (1926, 1931, etc.): institutes in both of the Americas;
5. In the fifth year (1927, 1932, etc.): institutes in other regions of the world, as well as societies of the common life without public vows.

The decree repeated the provision of canon 510 that if any congregation had a stipulation in its constitutions which, if approved after the promulgation of the Code, required a more frequent report, then the constitutions were to be followed rather than the decree.

Superiors general of institutes which became newly obliged by canon 510 to send a report were directed, until the Sacred Congregation should provide otherwise, to draw up a complete and truthful report on the state of their institute in such a manner as seemed best suited to the institute. The decree stated that this was an obligation binding in conscience. It was imposed that the Holy See might acquire a full knowledge of the material, moral, and disciplinary status of the institute.

Institutes of simple vows, which were required before the Code to make a report, were now to use the set of questions revised and published by the Sacred Congregation of Religious. [6] This revised formula contained 105 questions. Over and beyond these questions, the first report was to contain information concerning the history of the order or congregation and of its approbation by the Holy See. The internal form of government and the nature of the vows taken in the institute were also to be explained. If any change had been made in these matters from the time of foundation, this change was to be noted, as well as any relaxation in the observance of the rule, with the further indication of responsibility for such changes or relaxation as may have been made.

[6] S. Cong. de Rel., instr. 25 mart. 1922—*AAS*, XIV (1922), 278-286 (Latin text); *AAS*, XV (1923), 459-466, and *CLD*, I, 284-293 (English text).

After seven general questions by way of preamble, the other 98 questions were arranged under three categories, which pertained to persons, material goods, and religious discipline. The category concerning persons was divided into questions about postulants, novices, professed religious, and dismissed religious. The section on material goods was divided into questions on the individual religious houses and on the finances of the institute as a whole. The third category concerned religious discipline, and inquired into the state of religious observance in general as well as the observance of certain special laws, and, finally, into the external works of the institute.

Article III. The decree *Cum transactis*

The decree *Sancitum est* and the Instruction of March 25, 1922, with its list of questions, remained in force for 25 years. On July 9, 1947, the Sacred Congregation of Religious issued a new decree concerning the quinquennial report, entitled *Cum transactis.* [7] Subsequently, on December 9, 1948, three separate formulas of questions were issued by the same Congregation. [8]

Section 1. The Text of the Decree [9]

Concerning the Quinquennial Report which is to be made by Religious Institutes, Societies of the Common Life and Secular Institutes.

As more than twenty-five years have passed since the publication of the Decree, *Sancitum est,* of March 8, 1922, regulating the quinquennial report which is to be sent to the Holy See by the General Superiors of religious Institutes (c. 510), and as experience has clearly shown which of its provisions seem to merit definitive confirmation, what should be added to them,

[7] *AAS,* XL (1948), 378-381.

[8] These questionnaires were not published in the *AAS.* Cf. infra, pp. 43-44.

[9] The text presented here is taken verbatim from the translation supplied by the Sacred Congregation of Religious in the appendix to *The List of Questions Which are to be Answered by Religious Institutes and Societies in the Report to be Sent to the Holy See every Five Years according to the Decree "Cum transactis,"* For Religious Institutes and Societies of Pontifical Right (Rome: Polyglot Printing Press, 1957), pp. 33-36.

and which ones should be revoked or amended, as that Decree itself intimated, the Sacred Congregation of Religious, in the plenary session of the Eminent Fathers of July 4, 1947, decided to provide as follows:

I. According to the Code (c. 510), the Abbot Primate, the Abbot Superior of a monastic Congregation (c. 488, 8°), the Superior General of every religious Institute, Society of Common life without public vows (c. 675) and secular Institute [10] of pontifical right, and the President of any Federation of houses of religious Institutes, Societies of common life or secular Institutes, [11] and, in default of the above-named persons or if they are prevented from acting, their Vicars (c. 488, 8°), must send to the Holy See, that is to this Sacred Congregation of Religious, a report on the state of their religious Institute, Society, secular Institute or Federation, every five years, [12] even if the year assigned for sending the report falls wholly or partly within the first two years from the time when they entered upon the office.

II. The five-year periods shall be fixed and common to all those mentioned above in n. I; and they shall continue to be computed from the first day of January, 1923.

III. In making the reports the following order shall be observed:

[10] The addition of secular institutes reflects a new form of a canonical state of perfection developed since the promulgation of the Code. Secular institutes were authorized and recommended by Pope Pius XII in his Constitution *Provida Mater Ecclesia*, 2 febr. 1947—*AAS*, XXXIX (1947), 114-124; *CLD*, III, 135-146. The same constitution contains special statutes for such institutes.

[11] The addition of these federations reflects a new form of the organization of institutes which developed since the promulgation of the Code. Pope Pius XII urged, but did not make mandatory, the formation of federations of autonomous monasteries of nuns in his Constitution *Sponsa Christi*, 2 nov. 1950.—*AAS*, XLIII (1951), 5-21; *CLD*. III, 221-239. This constitution also promulgated general statutes for nuns.

[12] The decree omits all mention of that provision of canon 510 which stated that the report should be sent in more often than every five years if the constitutions so direct. This is an indication that the Sacred Congregation does not wish the report to be submitted oftener than at five-year intervals. On this point, cf. Creusen-Ellis, *Religious Men and Women in Church Law* (6th English ed., Milwaukee: The Bruce Publishing Company, 1958), p. 71.

1° From among the religious Institutes, Societies of common life, secular Institutes and Federations of pontifical right, whose members are men, the report is to be sent:

in the first year of the five-year period: by the Canons Regular, Monks and military Orders;

in the second year: by the Mendicants, Clerics Regular and other Regulars;

in the third year: by the clerical Congregations;

in the fourth year: by the Lay Congregations;

in the fifth year: by the Societies of common life, secular Institutes and Federations. [13]

2° From among the religious Institutes, Societies of common life, secular Institutes and Federations of pontifical right, whose members are women, the report is to be sent, according to the region in which the principal house is juridically established:

in the first year of the five-year period: by the Superioresses of religious Institutes in Italy, Spain and Portugal;

in the second year: by the Superioresses of religious Institutes in France, Belgium, Holland, England and Ireland;

in the third year: by the Superioresses of religious Institutes in other parts of Europe;

in the fourth year: by the Superioresses of religious Institutes in the countries of America;

in the fifth year: by the Superioresses of religious Institutes in other parts of the world, and moreover by the Superioresses of Societies of common life, secular Institutes and Federations throughout the world.

IV. In order that the Sacred Congregation may be able to obtain certain and authentic information regarding all those monasteries and independent houses of pontifical right, of both men and women, which are not bound by canon 510 to send the quinquiennal report, [14] and also regarding Congrega-

[13] It will be noted that for institutes of men the order for submitting the report has been slightly changed from the order prescribed by the decree *Sancitum est*. Cf. *supra*, p. 36.

[14] It will be noted that in n. IV. the decree imposes the obligation of sending a quinquennial report upon superiors of institutes which were not bound to do so by canon 510, namely, upon major superiors of independent monasteries of men and of nuns; upon general superiors of congregations, societies of common life and secular institutes of diocesan right; and upon superiors of independent religious houses and independent houses of a society without vows or of a secular institute, whether they be of pontifical or diocesan right.

tions, Societies of common life and secular Institutes, of diocesan right, the following are to be observed:

1° Major Superiors of monasteries or independent houses of men which, although they are of pontifical right, neither belong to any monastic Congregation nor are federated with others, shall send to the Ordinary of the place, at the time and in the order mentioned above (n. III, 1°), a summary report of the five-year period, signed by themselves and by their proper Councillors. The Ordinary in turn shall send a copy of this report, signed by himself, with any remarks he may see fit to add, to this Sacred Congregation within the year in which the report was made.

2° Major Superioresses of monasteries of nuns, with their proper Council, according to the order above prescribed (n. III, 2°) for General Superioresses, shall send a brief and concise report of the five-year period, signed by all of them, to the Ordinary of the place if the nuns are subject to him, otherwise to the Regular Superior. The Ordinary of the place or the Regular Superior shall carefully transmit a copy of the report, signed by himself and adding any remarks he may see fit to make, to this Sacred Congregation within the year in which the report was made.

3° The General Superiors of Congregations, Societies of common life and secular Institutes, of diocesan right, shall send a quinquennial report signed by themselves and by their proper Council, to the Ordinary of the place where the principal house is, at the time and in the order above prescribed (n. III, 1° and 2°). The Ordinary of the place shall not fail to communicate this report to the Ordinaries of the other houses, and he shall within the year send to this Sacred Congregation a copy signed by himself, and adding his own judgement and that of the other Ordinaries regarding the Congregation, Society or secular Institute in question.

4° Independent and autonomous religious houses and houses of a Society without vows or of a secular Institute, which are not united in a Federation, whether they be of diocesan or of pontifical right, shall send a summary report of the five-year period to the Ordinary of the place, in the order above prescribed (n. III, 1° and 2°). The Ordinary in turn shall send a copy of the said report, signed by himself, with any remarks he may see fit to make, to this Sacred Congregation, likewise within the year.

V. In making out their reports, all religious Institutes, monastic Congregations, Societies of common life, secular Institutes and Federations, of pontifical right, even though they be exempt, must follow exactly the schedule of questions which will be made out by the Sacred Congregation and sent to them directly.

Monasteries of nuns, autonomous houses of religious Institutes and of Societies and secular Institutes of pontifical right, and Congregations, Societies and secular Institutes of diocesan right, shall use shorter formulas which will be approved for them.

VI. The replies given to the questions proposed must always be sincere and as far as possible complete and based on careful inquiry; and this is an obligation in conscience according to the gravity of the matter. If eth replies are deficient in necessary matters, or if they seem uncertain or not sufficiently reliable, the Sacred Congregation will *ex officio* see to it that they are completed, and if need be will even itself directly conduct the investigations.

VII. Before the report is officially signed by the Superior and by the individual Councillors or Assistants, it is to be carefully examined personally and collectively.

The General Superioress of religious Institutes of women, and of Societies of common life, secular Institutes and Federations, of pontifical right, shall send the report, signed by herself and by her Council to the Ordinary of the place of the Generalate house so that he, according to law (c. 510) may sign the report; she shall then in due time see that the report signed by the Ordinary of the place is sent to this Sacred Congregation.

VIII. If any of the Superiors or Councillors who have to sign the report has any objection of any consequence to make to it, which he was not able to express in giving his vote, or if he judges that anything concerning the report should in any way be communicated to the Sacred Congregation, he may do this by a private letter, and may even be in conscience bound to do so according to the case. However, let him be mindful of his own condition and remember that he will gravely burden his conscience if he dares to state in such a secret letter anything which is not true.

IX. At the end of each year, all religious Institutes, Societies of common life, secular Institutes and Federations, whether of diocesan or pontifical right shall send directly to the Sacred Congregation of Religious the annual prospectuses according to the schedules contained in the formulas which will be made out and distributed by the Sacred Congregation stating the principal matters which concern the state of persons, works or other things which should be of interest either to the Sacred Congregation or to Superiors.

His Holiness Pius XII, in the Audience given to the undersigned Secretary of the Sacred Congregation of Religious on July 9, 1947, approved the text of this Decree and ordered that it be observed by all and that it be published, all things to the contrary notwithstanding.

Fr. L. H. Pasetto, Secretary

Section 2. The Lists of Questions

Number V of the decree *Cum transactis* specifies that in making the report all institutes follow one of the various formulas of questions made out by the Sacred Congregation itself. There are three lists of questions: one for institutes and societies of pontifical approval; one for diocesan institutes and societies; and one for independent houses. [15] Thus a change has been made from the prescription of the decree *Sancitum est,* which required the use of the earlier list of questions only on the part of religious institutes of

[15] These formulas of questions were drawn up by the Sacred Congregation, all under the same date of December 9, 1948. These formulas were not published in the *Acta Apostolicae Sedis,* but may be obtained from the Archivist, Sacred Congregation of Religious, Piazza Pio XII, 3, Rome, Italy.

Of the list of questions to be answered by institutes and societies of pontifical approval, Latin, English, Italian, French, German and Spanish versions are available from the Sacred Congregation. The English version may also be found in the *Canon Law Digest,* III, 162-201; and in *Review for Religious,* IX (1950), pp. 52-56, 108-112, 166-168, 209-224, 269-278. Modern language versions of the other two formulas are not available from the Sacred Congregation. However, an English version of the questions to be answered by diocesan institutes will be found in Creusen-Ellis, *Religious Men and Women in Church Law,* Appendix III, pp. 296-333. For the most part the questions are the same as those to be used by institutes of pontifical approval. And the *Canon Law Digest,* III, 204-205, contains a concordance of the simple vows which before the Code had been bound to make a report.[16]

The list of questions to be answered by pontifical institutes contains 342 inquiries. These are arranged under three chapters: I. Concerning the Institute and its Government; II. Concerning the Religious and the Religious Life and Discipline; III. Concerning the Works and Ministries of the Institute. The chapters are divided into articles, which in turn are subdivided. The same arrangement and divisions are found in the schedules of questions for diocesan institutes and for independent religious houses. The former has 322 questions; the latter, 171 questions.

Each of the three documents is preceded by points of which note is to be taken in the drawing up of the report. These points cover practical details for the answering of the questions, as well as a list of documents which should be sent to the Holy See, either at the time of the first reports, or in other stated circumstances.[17]

---

three questionnaires, so that the one English version available from the Sacred Congregation can easily be used by the other two groups, especially since the same volume of the *Canon Law Digest*, pp. 206-207, lists for diocesan institutes and for independent monasteries and houses those questions which do not appear in the questionnaire for institutes of pontifical approval.

16 Cf. *supra*, p. 37.

17 Further practical instructions on filling out the report can be found in an article by Fr. Adam C. Ellis, S.J., "Quinquennial Report, 1951," in *Review for Religious*, X (1951), 20-24. Fr. Ellis also published an article on the annual statistical reports that are required by the decree *Cum transactis*. Cf. "First Annual Report," in *Review for Religious*, IX (1950), 309-316. Consideration of the annual statistical report has been omitted from the present study as being beyond its scope. A circular letter of the Sacred Congregation of Religious, dated Feb. 9, 1950, but not published in the *Acta Apostolicae Sedis*, contains rather complete directions for filling out the annual statistical report. This letter is reproduced in *Canon Law Digest*, III, 207-212.

Also omitted from this study, on the score that it would unduly broaden its scope and contribute nothing additional to its primary purpose, is a consideration of the report required of institutes dependent on it by the Sacred Congregation for the Propagation of the Faith. This Instruction, dated June 29, 1937, will be found in *Sylloge Praecipuorum Documentorum Recentium Summorum Pontificum et S. Congregationis de Propaganda Fide necnon Aliarum SS. Congregationum Romanarum ad usum Missionariorum* (Romae: Typis Polyglottis Vaticanis, 1939), n. 225, pp. 656-667.

CHAPTER V

THE QUINQUENNIAL REPORT AS AN INSTRUMENT OF PAPAL SUPERVISION

The primary purpose of the quinquennial report is to provide accurate information to the Holy See, so that it may be able to "promote what is good, and correct what is wrong." [1] It is, then, an instrument of supervision on the part of the Holy See, and it is with relation to this concept that the report will be examined in this chapter.

ARTICLE I. OBEDIENCE OF RELIGIOUS TO THE HOLY SEE

Under the term "Holy See" the Code of Canon Law includes the Roman Congregations, Tribunals and Offices, as well as the Roman Pontiff himself. [2] Pertinent to this study is a consideration of the obedience due on the part of religious to the Roman Pontiff and to the Sacred Congregation of Religious.

Religious are subject to the Holy Father just as the rest of the faithful. Moreover, they are subject to him in a special way as religious, in that he is their highest superior to whom obedience in virtue of the vow is due. [3] Were occasion to arise for the Holy Father to oblige religious in virtue of their vow, he would be restricted, like other superiors, to the matter of the vow. For the vow of obedience itself extends only to commands made according to the rule and constitutions. Superiors invoking the vow of

[1] Pius XII, allocutio, 9 dec. 1957—*AAS*, L (1958), 42; *CLD, Supplement through 1960*, can. 487, p. 16.

[2] Can. 7.

[3] Can. 499, § 1.

obedience call upon dominative power over their subjects, which is a result of the religious profession of the subjects, made in accordance with the rule and constitutions. Therefore, the Holy Father cannot impose obligations to be fulfilled in virtue of the vow if these commands are beyond the scope of the religious rule and constitutions. [4] He can, however, by reason of his supreme power of jurisdiction [5] impose obligations which go beyond the rule or constitutions; but such obligations do not bind in virtue of the vow of obedience.

Like other members of the Church, religious owe obedience to the Sacred Congregations of the Roman Curia. In view of their state, however, they owe a special religious obedience to the Sacred Congregation of Religious, which enjoys the status of a superior over them. [6] It is probable that the Sacred Congregation of Religious may oblige religious under the vow of obedience without a particular delegation from the Holy Father. [7] In any case, however, it is not presumed that the pope or the Sacred Congregation commands in virtue of the vow; rather, such an intention must be clear, and must be determined from the wording of the command, the matter involved, or the circumstances of the precept. This principle applies to all superior-subject relationships of religious in so far as an obligation under the vow of obedience is concerned. [8]

[4] Schaefer, *De Religiosis* (4. ed., Romae: Editrice "Apostolato Cattolico," 1947), p. 158, n. 362; Coronata, *Institutiones Iuris Canonici* (2. ed., 5 vols., Taurini: Marietti, 1939-1947), I, ed. altera et emendata, 1939, p. 641, n. 528. In his 4th edition, 1950, Coronata omits this observation. Future citations will point to the second edition.

[5] Cf. can. 218, § 1: "Romanus Pontifex, Beati Petri in primatu Successor, habet non solum primatum honoris, sed supremam et plenam potestatem iurisdictionis in universam Ecclesiam tum in rebus quae ad fidem et mores, tum in iis quae ad disciplinam et regimen Ecclesiae per totum orbem diffusae pertinent."

[6] Schaefer, *De Religiosis*, p. 159, n. 364.

[7] Schaefer, *ibid.*, p. 162, n. 369; Coronata, *op. cit.*, p. 642, n. 528; Larraona, "Commentarium Codicis," *CpR*, VI (1925), 81.

[8] Cf. Schaefer, *loc. cit.*; Coronata, *loc. cit.*

Article II. The force of *Cum transactis*

It is of no little importance to determine the obligatory force of the decree *Cum transactis*, and to specify the precise juridical basis of its binding power. The importance of such a determination can be seen from three factors: (1) the decree not only applies canon 510, but also induces certain obligations independently of that canon; (2) the decree suggests the existence of certain obligations beyond the ones specified by the canons of the Code; (3) the decree indirectly, at least, interprets somes canons of the Code. [9]

If the decree merely applied the prescriptions of canon 510 to specific circumstances there would be no problem. For Pope Benedict XV drastically restricted the legislative power of the Congregations of the Roman Curia. They are not to enact new legislation unless some serious need concerning the good of the whole Church demands it. In that eventuality, their decree is to be approved by the Supreme Pontiff himself as a new law; and it is to be inserted into the Code by the Pontifical Commission for the Authentic Interpretation of the Canons of the Code. Aside from this eventuality it is the task of the Congregations to insure the conscientious observance of the prescriptions of the Code, and to issue instructions which furnish greater clarity to the laws of the Code and render them more effectual. [10] These instructions or decrees are primarily administrative measures calculated to apply the law to concrete circumstances, or to regulate conditions in accordance with the Code. [11]

If the decree *Cum transactis* fulfilled this function alone, there would be no further need to explore its nature. But, as has been mentioned, this decree adds a new obligation to canon 510, an addition which can in no sense be described as applying the Code

[9] Each of these three factors is further discussed elsewhere in this study. Cf. pp. 47-48, 57-76, 90-97.

[10] Motu propr. *Cum iuris canonici*, 15 sept. 1917 — *AAS*, IX (1917), 483-484.

[11] Schmidt, *The Principles of Authentic Interpretation in Canon 17 of the Code of Canon Law*, The Catholic University of America Canon Law Studies, No. 141 (Washington, D.C.: The Catholic University of America Press, 1941), pp. 83-84.

to a particular circumstance. For the decree increases the categories of superiors who are to submit a quinquennial report. [12] Such an enlargement of the scope of canon 510 definitely goes beyond the mere application of the canon to concrete circumstances. An entirely new obligation has been added. It remains, then, to consider what is the basis of this obligation, and what is its force.

The wording of the decree does not justify an assertion that it obliges preceptively by virtue of the vow of obedience. Even though some authors acknowledge for the Sacred Congregation of Religious, by reason of its ordinary power, the right to bind religious in virtue of their vow of obedience, it seems that such an intention should not simply be presumed in regard to the binding force of the decree *Cum transactis*. Likewise, there is no basis in the wording of the decree for asserting that it obliges preceptively in virtue of the vow of obedience by reason of the special authorization of the Holy Father. [13] And, although the decree was approved by the Holy Father, [14] this approval did not transform it from a decree of the Sacred Congregation to a pontifical law or precept. The fact that it does not bind strictly as a law, nor in virtue of the vow of obedience, does not, however, exclude all binding character from it. This fact is evident, both from the

[12] Cf. *Cum transactis*, nn., I, IV. Cf. *supra*, pp. 40-41.

[13] Writing for nuns, Gutiérrez comments: "Le risposte al presente questionario devono essere fatte... con spirito di sottomissione. Il Papa è il primo Superiore dei Religiosi. Tutti, anche gli stessi Superiori, in quanto tali, gli sono soggetti in virtù del voto di obbedienza (can. 499, § 1). " — Larraona ed altri collaboratori, *La Nuova Disciplina Canonica sulle Monache* (Roma: Desclée e C., 1952), Gutiérrez, "Della Relatione Quinquennale da Farsi alla Santa Sede," p. 235.

Gutiérrez does not say here explicitly that the obligation to answer the questions in a spirit of submission is an obligation binding under the vow of obedience. In view of the limited canonical background his intended readers may be presumed to possess, however, it is unfortunate that he did not further qualify his remarks.

[14] "Sanctissimus Dominus Noster Pius PP. XII, in Audientia habita ab infrascripto Secretario Sacrae Congregationis de Religiosis, die 9 Iulii 1947, praesentis Decreti tenorem approbavit et ab omnibus servari et publici iuris fieri mandavit, contrariis quibuscumque non obstantibus."— *Cum transactis*, n. IX.

wording of the pontifical approbation and from the statement of the decree itself, that it obliges in conscience.[15]

In order, then, to establish the binding force of the decree *Cum transactis*, one must show that it is an ordinance whose binding force rests neither on legislative power nor on the power to oblige in virtue of the vow of obedience. Such an ordinance is verified in the notion of a common precept. A precept can be defined as a command directed by a competent superior either to individual persons or to a community.[16] A precept is called jurisdictional if it emanates from the jurisdictional power of a superior; it is called dominative if it is imposed in virtue of purely administrative power. If the precept is addressed to an entire community or to an entire class of subjects it is called a common precept; if addressed to individuals, it is termed a particular precept.[17] All the acts by which a superior applies or executes laws in virtue of his administrative power can rightly be called precepts.[18] If this administrative power derives from the power of jurisdiction, the precept will be a jurisdictional precept. Ecclesiastical jurisdiction is the public power granted by Christ to the Church to govern the faithful.[19] The Roman Pontiff has supreme jurisdiction in the whole Church,[20] and the Roman Congregations partake in

[15] "Responsa propositis quaestionibus danda, onerata pro rei gravitate conscientia, sincera semper sint atque, accuratis praemissis informationibus, pro viribus completa." — *Cum transactis*, n. VI.

[16] Cf. Beste, *Introductio in Codicem* (4. ed., Neapoli: M. D'Auria, 1956), p. 92; Van Hove, *Commentarium in Codicem Iuris Canonici*, Vol. I, Tom. II, *De Legibus Ecclesiasticis* (Mechliniae-Romae: H. Dessain, 1930), p. 360, n. 353; Coronata, *Institutiones Iuris Canonici*, I, p. 47, n. 31.

[17] Beste, *loc. cit.* It would be irrelevant to the scope of the present study to discuss the divergence of opinions among the authors on the precise nature of the common precept. While admitting the validity of the term, some authors hold that a common precept is in reality a particular precept imposed on many individuals. Cf. Michiels, *Normae Generales Juris Canonici* (2. ed., 2 vols., Parisiis-Tornaci-Romae: Desclée et Socii, 1949), I, 694-698; Van Hove, *ibid.*, p. 111, n. 101, and p. 373, n. 369; Roelker, *Precepts* (Paterson, New Jersey: St. Anthony Guild Press, 1955), pp. 39-41.

[18] Van Hove, *ibid.*, p. 372, n. 368.

[19] Coronata, *Institutiones Iuris Canonici*, I, p. 329, n. 276.

[20] Can. 218, § 1.

this jurisdiction.[21] Therefore the jurisdictional power attributed to the individual Congregations is truly pontifical in character; it is also ordinary, in so far as it is attributed to the Congregations by the law itself.[22]

It can be concluded, therefore, that the commands of the Sacred Congregation of Religious are jurisdictional precepts. And the decree *Cum transactis* can rightly be called a common precept, jurisdictional in character, emanating from the administrative power with which the Sacred Congregation is endowed. By virtue of the power of jurisdiction of the Sacred Congregation, those to whom the decree is directed have the corresponding obligation to observe it.

The decree specifically directs superiors who must compile the quinquennial report to make an accurate investigation of the facts and to furnish responses that are sincere, and complete. This is an obligation in conscience, according to the gravity of the matter.[23]

The phrase "*onerata pro rei gravitate conscientia,*" stated in terms of moral theology, implies an obligation which is grave *in genere suo*, but which admits of parvity of matter. An insincere or incomplete answer in regard to a point of smaller moment would hardly be considered a matter of serious consequence. For example, Question 35 inquires about the time and manner in which the superior general promulgated the decree and decisions of the general chapter. If the response contained a mistake in regard to the date, this would not be a serious defect, even if the error were the result of culpable carelessness. But the case might be different in regard to Question 36, which inquires whether, in the promulgation of the aforesaid decrees, anything was omitted, and if so, what was the reason for the omission. If the general superior had

21 The wording of the title of the Code under which the canons on the Roman Congregations are placed is: "De Suprema potestate deque iis qui eiusdem sunt ecclesiastico iure participes" —Liber II, Pars I, Sectio II, Tit. VII.

22 Sheehy, *The Sacred Congregation of the Sacraments*, The Catholic University of America Canon Law Studies, No. 333 (Washington, D.C.: The Catholic University of America Press, 1954), p. 111.

23 *Cum transactis*, n. VI.

suppressed a decree of the general chapter by not promulgating it, an insincere or untruthful answer to Question 36 would be an example of a serious failure to obey the decree *Cum transactis.* Even if the general superior had a justifying reason for the suppression of the decree, the Sacred Congregation has a right to know both the fact of the suppression and the reason for it.

ARTICLE III. PAPAL SUPERVISION THROUGH THE REPORT

It has been seen above that the primary purpose of the quinquennial report is to provide accurate information to the Holy See. The purpose underlying the acquisition of such information is to enable the Holy See to supervise religious through guidance, instructions and directives. [24]

The information garnered from the quinquennial report is comprehensive and detailed. Its comprehensiveness can be seen both from the documents required to be sent with the report, [25] and from a study of the questions themselves. A description of

[24] S. C. Ep. et Reg., decr. *In approbandis,* 16 iul. 1906: "Huiusmodi enim relatione singula Instituta, quorum domus in variis exstant dioecesibus dissitisque locis, explorata perspectaque fiunt eidem S. Sedi; quae idcirco continua providentia ea prosequi et, si quando a legibus deflectere videantur, sive cohortationibus sive correctionibus mandatisque ad pristinam observationem revocare potest." — *Fontes,* IV, n. 2052.

[25] Included among the documents are: the constitutions; compendiums of privileges; special laws; books of customs; liturgical books and prayerbooks; statutes governing religious and clerical training; statutes for affiliated tertiaries or oblates; formularies used for the appointment to offices, or for making visitation reports; copies of the principal books which show the spirit, way of life, history and activities of the institute. Also required is a historico-juridical account of the institute. All of the documents just mentioned were to be sent in only with the first report following the issuance of the 1948 List of Questions. Also to be sent, as soon as they appear, or at least with the next quinquennial report, are the official commentaries of the institute; the minutes of the general chapter; instructions, ordinances, and other important documents of the superior general. — *Elenchus Quaestionum quibus a Religionibus et Societatibus in Relatione ad Sanctam Sedem Quinto Quoque Anno Transmittenda Est ad Normam Decreti Cum Transactis: pro Religionibus et Societatibus Iuris Pontificii* (Romae: Typis Polyglottis Vaticanis, 1949), "Animadvertenda," B),

the details covered by the questions would be tantamount to a reproduction of the 342 questions themselves. But an outline of the subject matter of the questions, based upon headings in the text, is presented here to illustrate the scope of the report.

Chapter I: The Institute and its Government.
Article I: Concerning the Institute in general.
§ 1. The institute in general: the special end; second Orders, congregations, societies, institutes of women which are subject to the institute or society.
§ 2. The internal organization and division of the institute: assistancies and congregations; provinces, vice-provinces and other equivalent units; the houses.

Article II: Concerning the juridical government of the institute: the general government; the general chapter, its convocation and session; promulgation and execution; appointments to offices; the duties of superiors: residence; making known and observing the decrees of the Holy See; the canonical visitation; freedom of epistolary correspondence; council meetings; corrections and the abuse of power; the exercise of authority; relations with the ordinaries of places.

Article III: Concerning the spiritual government of the institute: confessors; spiritual direction; the reception of the Most Blessed Eucharist.

Article IV: Concerning the financial government of the institute.
§ 1. Concerning the acquisition and loss of property: the acquisition and registration of property; expenses; the alienation or diminution of property; debts and obligations.
§ 2. The conservation and administration of property: the rendering of accounts; the investment of money and changes of investment; the conservation of property; foundations, pious causes; business, trade; actions or affairs which involve financial responsibility.

---

pp. 3–4 (hereafter cited *Elenchus Quaestionum*). — It should be noted that the "*Animadvertenda*" differ in the three versions of the questions; namely, the versions for pontifical institutes, for independent monasteries or houses, and for diocesan institutes.

Chapter II: The Religious and the Religious Life and Discipline.

Article I: Concerning the admission, formation and profession or incorporation of members: the postulantship in the wide sense (apostolic schools) ; the postulantship in the canonical or strict sense; the admission of aspirants; documents, testimonials and informations; impediments and admission; the noviceship: the houses; the beginnings of the noviceship; board and expenses for the postulantship and the noviceship; the discipline of the noviceship; the government of the noviceship; the spiritual training of the novices; the documents to be drawn up before profession; the admission to profession and the act of profession; the canonical examination; the obligation and delivery of the dowry; the investment, conservation, administration and return of the dowry; the profession and the renewal of profession; solemn profession.

Article II: Concerning the religious life and discipline: the vows; poverty and the common life; chastity and its safeguards; obedience; the Rule and constitutions; the religious habit; exercises of piety; choir service and the divine Office; religious charity; the reading of books.

Article III: Concerning those who have departed or have been dismissed; those who have gone out from the institute; apostates and fugitives; those dismissed by superiors, and those sent back to the world; those who were excloistered; absences from the house; the deceased.

Article IV: Concerning the various classes and conditions of religious.

§ 1. Concerning clerics.[26]

§ 2. *Conversi* or coadjutors: their education and training.

§ 3. Religious in military service: the profession of those who are to be called for the first time to active military service; the religious during their military service; the renewal of temporary profession after military service and the making of perpetual profession.

Chapter III: The Works and Ministries of the Institute.

Article I: Concerning ministries in general: the special end and the works of the institute in general; abuses in the exercise

[26] There are no questions under this heading. Cf. *infra*, pp. 55-56.

of ministries; difficulties with the secular clergy or with other institutes, etc., because of the ministries.

Article II: Concerning special ministries: missions among infidels and heretics; parishes, churches and sanctuaries; colleges, schools and seminaries; the practice of the corporal works of mercy; the apostolate of the press; Catholic Action; priestly administrations; the celebration of the Holy Sacrifice, and Mass stipends and obligations; domestic services.

Conclusion: A summary comparative judgment regarding the state of the institute, concerning striving toward perfection, the state of discipline, the economic condition, the special end and works.

The scope of the quinquennial report can also be inferred from the number of canons referred to in the questions. Explicit reference is made to 110 of the 194 canons of the Code of Canon Law which comprise the section *De Religiosis.*[27] In addition, reference is made to 37 canons in other sections of the Code.

With answers to such a comprehensive list of questions, the Holy See has extremely detailed information on the various facets of religious life in each institute. This information is then employed by the Congregation as a basis for its supervision of religious. Supervision formulated upon the information gained from the quinquennial report can be directed to the institute submitting the report. Or the information can be used even further, as an aid in formulating instructions or decrees for religious in general.

The decree *Cum transactis* itself intimates the manner in which the report serves as a basis for supervision of the institute which submitted it. The decree states:

> If the replies are deficient in necessary matters, or if they seem uncertain or not sufficiently reliable, the Sacred Congregation will *ex officio* see to it that they are completed, and if need be will even itself directly conduct the investigation.[28]

[27] That is, cc. 487-681.

[28] *Cum transactis*, n. VI.

Moreover, Question one of the formulary, referring to the immediately preceding report asks:

> b) Whether, and when, a reply was received from the Sacred Congregation.
> c) Whether the observations (*animadversiones*) which may have been made by the Sacred Congregation upon the report were faithfully carried out in practice.

This question indicates that the practice of the Holy See is to send "observations" based upon the report to the respective institutes. These observations are to be "faithfully carried out." [29]

These reports are not only a basis for individual supervision, but also serve as reference guides for general instructions or decrees for religious. [30] These instructions or decrees may seek to implement observance of the canons of the Code; [31] they may also strive to unify or direct efforts of various institutes for the greater good of the Church and of souls. [32]

If the report is such a basic instrument of supervision, one may ask why there are no questions concerning the training of clerical religious. Chapter II, Article IV, § 1, of the List of Questions is entitled "Concerning Clerics." Yet under that heading there are no questions, but merely the statement that "this is dealt with in the report on formation and studies." This omission does not indicate that the Holy See considers supervision in the area of clerical training to be of little importance. At the time of the

29 That such observations are actually sent is verified by the experience of general superiors. and affirmed to the present writer by the Very Reverend Elio Gambari, S.M.M., a member of the Sacred Congregation of Religious and co-author of the List of Questions.

30 This use of the quinquennial report is implied by Pugliese, who is a member of the Sacred Congregation of Religious: "Omnes qui aliquo modo in Ecclesia latina publicam professionem faciunt religiosae perfectionis, S. C. de Religiosis plene et directe subiiciuntur, cuius est igitur de eis inquirere, eosque defendere, et, si casus ferat, arguere aut de eis quomodocumque *legiferare*" (emphasis added). — "Adnotationes de Quinquennali Relatione a Religionibus, a Societatibus Vitae Communis et ab Institutibus Saecularibus Facienda," *Monitor Ecclesiasticus*, LXXV (1950), 197.

31 Cf. Benedict XV, *Cum iuris canonici*, n. II — *AAS*, IX (1917), 483.

32 Cf. Pugliese, "art. cit.," *ibid.*, pp. 191-193, 196.

publication of the List of Questions for the quinquennial report in 1948, the Sacred Congregation was preparing statutes which would govern the religious, clerical and apostolic training of religious studying for the priesthood. The results of this preparation are embodied in Pius XII's Constitution *Sedes Sapientiae* [33] and in the General Statutes promulgated by that constitution. [34]

This legislation reorganized the entire program of studies and the training of clerical members of states of perfection, and instituted an unprecedented direct supervision of this phase of religious life. [35] No longer are schools for the clerical training of religious considered private institutions; they are recognized by the Holy See as official ecclesiastical schools, canonically on a par with diocesan seminaries. [36] The Sacred Congregation of Religious, though it already had jurisdiction over matters pertaining to the studies of religious, [37] was given a special mandate to take the initiative in supervising the training of clerics and to enforce the new General Statutes. [38] One of the means specified for supervising (*invigilandam*) and enforcing (*urgendam*) the execution of the General Statutes is a periodic report, which is to be made to the Sacred Congregation of Religious according to a formulary prepared by the Congregation. [39] The General Statutes explicitly mention the periodic report as a means of supervision. [40] This fact confirms the

[33] 31 maii 1956 — *AAS*, XLVIII (1956), 354-365.

[34] *Constitutio Apostolica* "*Sedes Sapientiae*" *eique adnexa* "*Statuta Generalia*" (2. ed., Romae: Apud Custodiam Librariam Sacrae Congregationis de Religiosis, 1957) (hereafter cited *Sedes Sapientiae*, or *Stat. Gen.*, respectively).

[35] Cf. Frison, "The Laws of Training in the Apostolic Constitution *Sedes Sapientiae*," — *The Jurist*, XXI (1961), 375-376.

[36] *Sedes Sapientiae*, n. 8; *Stat. Gen.*, art. 14. Cf. Frison, *ibid.*, p. 379.

[37] Can. 251, § 1.

[38] *Sedes Sapientiae*, n. 8, n. 40; *Stat. Gen.*, art. 18.

[39] *Stat. Gen.*, art. 18, § 2, 1°. This list of questions is now in preparation. And it will be a quinquennial report, timed to coincide with the more general report required by the decree *Cum transactis*. New instructions governing the training of lay brothers and of religious sisters are also under preparation. — Gutiérrez, "Introductio in Constitutionem Apostolicam 'Sedes Sapientiae'," — *CpRM*, XXXVII (1958), 39-40; Frison, "art. cit.," *The Jurist*, XXI (1961), 378.

[40] Art. 18.

statement that the more general quinquennial report required by the decree *Cum transactis* is also considered by the Holy See to be an instrument of the supervision of religious.

ARTICLE IV. THE REPORT AS A BASIS FOR DISCERNING THE MIND OF THE HOLY SEE

Since the questions in the quinquennial report are primarily intended as means of acquiring information, it cannot be said that each question indicates a new obligation imposed on religious. Nevertheless, emanating as they do from the Sacred Congregation, these questions are expressions of the *stylus* or *praxis* of the Congregation. Therefore it has been correctly asserted that the questions manifest the mind of the Holy See in regard to the government, the administration and the principal obligations of religious.[41]

Many of the questions in the quiquennial report imply the existence of certain obligations for religious that are not mentioned in the Code of Canon Law. Some of these points are found in the *Normae* of 1901,[42] and are therefore presumed to be in the constitutions of most institutes. But there are others which are found neither in the Code nor in the *Normae*. The most important of these points the writer will discuss here, in order to show the development of the *stylus curiae* in regard to religious life during the period since the Code.[43]

Section 1. Religious Houses

Question 21 inquires:

In the erection and suppression of houses, were the rules of law (cc. 497, 498) and the standards of prudence observed,

[41] Creusen-Ellis, *Religious Men and Women in Church Law*, pp. 72-73; Larraona, "Commentarium Codicis," *CpR*, VIII (1927), p. 277, footnote (33).

[42] Cf. *supra*, p. 15.

[43] The questions here noted are all drawn from the List of Questions for pontifical institutes. Omitted from this article is any consideration of those topics which are considered at greater length in Chapter VIII, under the aspect of interpretation of the Code.

among which must be numbered a written contract, clear, complete and drawn up in accordance with canon law and the constitutions, with due regard to civil law.

The canons referred to in the question regulate the establishment or suppression of religious houses. The permission of the Holy See is needed for the establishing of houses for exempt religious, for nuns, or for religious institutes of any type if they are located in territory subject to the Sacred Congregation for the Propagation of the Faith. In addition, the written consent of the local ordinary is required. His consent suffices for the establishment of all other types of religious houses.[44] His written consent is also required for the erection of a school, a hospice, or any similar building which is separated from the religious house.[45]

The permission of the Holy See is necessary for the suppressing of a house of exempt religious. If a house belongs to a non-exempt institute of pontifical approval, it can be suppressed by the superior general with the consent of the local ordinary. If the house pertains to a diocesan congregation, it can be suppressed by the local ordinary after consultation with the superior general of the institute.[46]

The canons do not require that a contract be made between the local ordinary and the religious institute. In fact, nowhere in the Code, not even in the canons governing the union of parishes with religious communities,[47] is there a clear insistence that a contract be made. The written consent of the ordinary required by canon 497 is not necessarily a contract. In itself it does not verify the notion of a contract, which can be defined as the consent of two or more persons to the same proposition, manifested by a sensible sign and giving rise to an obligation in at least one of the parties contracting.[48] Nevertheless, it should not be concluded that Question 21 is introducing a new factor in the relationship

[44] Can. 497, § 1.

[45] Can. 497, § 3.

[46] Can. 498.

[47] Cf. cc. 452, 1423, 1425.

[48] Beste, *Introductio in Codicem*, p. 817.

of religious to local ordinaries. It is a well known fact that the Holy See wishes contracts to be entered into when religious assume charge of a parish, [49] or of other churches entrusted to them by the local ordinary, [50] and when they assume the direction of a diocesan seminary. [51] It is also customary for contractual agreements to be made when religious are placed in charge of parish schools, diocesan high schools and similar institutions, or when they assume the care of souls in mission territories. It is only by means of such contracts that the rights and obligations of both parties may be defined and future disputes obviated. Question 21, therefore, does not introduce a new obligation. Rather, it serves to remind superiors that it is the practice of the Holy See to require that these contracts be made. [52]

In regard to the physical structure of religious houses, Question 22, a), indicates that the Holy See wishes each religious to have a separate cell. If common dormitories are in use, each religious must at least have a bed set apart from the others.

Question 23 also reflects the mind of the Holy See when it inquires whether rooms for receiving guests are separate from that part of the house which is reserved to the community. [53]

Section 2. The General Chapter

Questions 26-28 make enquiries about matters pertaining to general chapters. In particular, Questions 30-37 indicate the mind

[49] Cf. *Elenchus Quaestionum*, q. 291. [50] Cf. *ibid.*, q. 294.

[51] Cf. *ibid.*, q. 296.

[52] Examples of contracts which can be used for the erection of a religious house, for the union of a parish with a religious institute, for the employment of religious in teaching, in social work, in hospitals and orphanages, can be found in Lynch, *Contracts between Bishops and Religious Congregations*, The Catholic University of America Canon Law Studies, No. 239 (Washington, D.C.: The Catholic University of America Press, 1946), pp. 195-201.

[53] In the Order of Friars Minor this requirement is interpreted to refer also to guests who are religious. Cf. *Regula et Constitutiones Generales Ordinis Fratrum Minorum*, art. 289, § 1: "In quolibet conventu mansiones sint cum necessaria supellectili, recipiendis hospitibus destinatae, a *cellis ceterorum* [emphasis added] religiosorum, in quantum fieri potest, separatae."

of the Holy See in their regard and imply the existence of obligations not specified in the Code. Thus it appears that each province is to present to the general chapter an accurate report on the condition of the province. A similar report on the state of the whole institute, drawn up by the general curia, should be seriously weighed and discussed by the chapter before the general elections. At the conclusion of the chapter the minutes are to be sent to the Sacred Congregation of Religious. The superior general with his council must faithfully promulgate and implement the decisions of the chapter.

Section 3. Unity among the Religious

The subject matter of Questions 67-69 is the promotion of unity among the members of the institute. While the Code makes community life a requisite of the religious state,[54] it does not lay down regulations for the fostering of community spirit and unity. The List of Questions suggests, by way of example, some means for fostering that unity. Thus it is asked if there are reports published about work done by members of the institute. It is indicated that bulletins issued by houses, provinces, or by the entire institute, are valuable means of fostering unity. It is suggested that a chronicle be kept and that in it be recorded the principal events of each house.

Section 4. Spiritual Life

In Article III of Chapter I, the List of Questions inquires about various aspects of the spiritual government of institutes. Within this section, Questions 80-85 contain, by implication, some new directives.

It is almost axiomatic to state that spiritual direction is a useful and almost necessary means for progress in the spiritual life. Spiritual direction can be described as instruction and encouragement

[54] Can. 487.

of individuals on the way of perfection, given by a competent adviser. The need for such direction has been stressed by ascetical writers of the past, by the Doctors of the Church, and by writers of the present day.[55] Although the Code of Canon Law does not contain legislation directly controlling spiritual direction for religious, it has been maintained that, at least for women religious, the Church wishes that the ordinary confessor[56] give spiritual direction. One of the arguments in favor of this contention is that the Code requires these confessors to be mature men, who are carefully selected on the basis of their outstanding prudence,[57] a fact which indicates that they should be able and willing to give direction. In addition, the law limiting their number[58] implies the desirability of uniformity of direction.[59] The writer subscribes to this view, and would add that it is supported by canon 520, § 2, which prescribes that, if a religious sister, for peace of mind or greater spiritual progress, desires a special confessor or *spiritual director*, the ordinary shall grant her request.

Nevertheless, the Code is silent about the training of spiritual directors, even though, as has been shown, it presumes that they will be available. Seemingly seeking to fill this lacuna in the Code, Question 80 indicates that superiors in clerical institutes should provide for the solid training of spiritual directors. Question 83 adds that superiors should promote spiritual direction for their subjects.

The Questions make an important addition to the requirements of canon 566, wherein it is prescribed that confessors reside in the novitiate of clerical institutes. The necessity of such residence is

55 Cf. Coogan. "Do We Need Direction ?" — *Review for Religious*, I (1942), 376-381.

56 Cf. can. 520, § 1: "Singulis religiosarum domibus unus dumtaxat detur confessarius ordinarius, qui sacramentales confessiones universae communitatis excipiat, nisi propter magnum ipsarum numerum vel aliam iustam causam sit opus altero vel pluribus."

57 Can. 524, § 1.

58 Can. 520, § 1.

59 Cf. "Spiritual Direction by the Ordinary Confessor," an editorial in *Review for Religious*, I (1942), 218-222.

now extended to all houses of study in these institutes, as Question 81 indicates. Furthermore, canon 566 speaks only of confessors; but the question refers to spiritual directors as well.[60]

Question 84 makes reference to canon 595, §§ 2-4. In this canon the Code directs superiors to promote frequent, and even daily, Communion among their subjects, always without prejudice to full liberty of conscience. The question inquires whether, in fulfilling this directive, superiors have followed the instructions of the Holy See. Thus Question 84 serves to remind superiors of the Instruction of the Sacred Congregation of the Sacraments on Daily Communion.[61] This Instruction puts appropriate emphasis on the full freedom the individual should enjoy in choosing to receive Holy Communion. It also directs that confessors be easily available for religious before the time for Holy Communion. Question 85 adverts to this prescription, and likewise inquires whether superiors allow their subjects a suitable time for preparation and thanksgiving in regard to this reception of Holy Communion.

Questions in other sections reflect the existence of further obligations on the part of superiors in the supervision of the spiritual life of their subjects. Thus it is indicated that superiors should strive to make it possible for all religious to attend community exercises.[62] But if a religious is absent from community exercises, the superior should arrange that he have time in which he can make up these exercises.[63] Moreover, the superior should make sure that the religious actually does fulfill this obligation.[64] Finally, superiors should be solicitous that the priests who are subject to them make a suitable preparation before Mass, that they celebrate devoutly and observe the rubrics, and that they make a proper thanksgiving after Mass.[65]

[60] "Utrum cura adhibeatur ut in Novitiatibus (c. 566, § 2) et etiam Collegiis omnibus, praescripti Confessarii et Directores spirituales habeantur et seligantur; et, si agatur de Religione clericali, ibidem commorentur (c. 566, § 2, 2º)."

[61] 8 dec. 1938. This instruction is not published in the *AAS*, but is found in *CLD*, II, 208-215.

[62] *Elenchus Quaestionum*, q. 238.

[63] *Ibid.*, q. 239.

[64] *Ibid.*, q. 240.

[65] *Ibid.*, q. 319.

Section 5. The Administration of Property

Article IV of Chapter II of the List of Questions pertains to the financial administration of religious institutes. The subject matter of the questions in this article corresponds, in a general way, to the canons of the Code which govern the administration of the temporal goods of religious.[66] The questions, however, serve to make known the mind of the Holy See on several points not treated in the Code.

Thus Questions 88 and 89 show that each institute, each province and each house should have an accurate inventory of its immovable[67] and movable[68] property, with an especial accounting of that property which in the law is designated as precious.[69] With regard to this inventory, Question 88 makes a parenthetical reference to canon 1522, 2°, a canon which, in turn, is complementary to canon 1521. According to the latter canon, if the law or articles of foundation have provided no administrator for the property of a church or of a pious foundation, then the local ordinary is to appoint a board of administration. Before the board begins to function, canon 1522, 2°, directs that an accurate inventory be made, which shall list all immovable property, all precious movable objects, and all other property. Moreover, the properties are to be described and an evaluation placed on them. For religious

[66] Can. 531-537.

[67] "Immovable goods are those which cannot without some alteration be transported from one place to another since they are rooted in the ground; for example, a house or a field." — Fanfani-O'Rourke, *Canon Law for Religious Women* (Dubuque, Iowa: The Priory Press, 1961), p. 129, n. 94.

[68] "Movable goods are those which may be transported from one place to another without changing their nature; for example, a table, clothing, grain or money." — Fanfani-O'Rourke, *loc. cit.*

[69] Can. 1497, § 2, describes as *precious* those objects which have a special intrinsic, artistic or historic value. Examples of such objects are valuable paintings, pieces of sculpture or tapestries; ancient codices, coins, special documents, or anything that has a notable value by reason of its antiquity or because of its association with a celebrated personage; or an object made of precious metal and adorned with gems. — Bouscaren-Ellis, *Canon Law, A Text and Commentary* (3. ed., Milwaukee: The Bruce Publishing Company, 1958), pp. 780-781.

institutes there is no need for the board of administration mentioned in canon 1521. The administration of the property of religious is to be governed by their constitutions, whereas the canon envisions a situation wherein no provision is made for temporal administration. Nevertheless, Question 88, by reason of its reference to canon 1522, 2°, implies that the position of religious administrators is analogous to that of the board of administration mentioned in canon 1521. And the question makes known that it is the mind of the Holy See that an inventory be made before religious administrators assume their office. In this inventory, property which does not belong to the religious institute, but which is connected with works entrusted to it, should be kept clearly distinct from the property of the community. [70]

Questions 101-105 are concerned with the alienation and diminution of property. Most of the obligations mentioned in these questions are already specified in the Code. Thus, reference is made to canons 534 [71] and 1531, [72] which outline the formalities required in the alienation of goods. Question 101 inquires whether any of the permanent assets of the institute have been alienated,

[70] *Elenchus Quaestionum*, q. 90.

[71] § 1. "Firmo praescripto can. 1531, si agatur de alienandis rebus pretiosis aliisve bonis quorum valor superet summam triginta millium francorum seu libellarum, vel de contrahendis debitis et obligationibus ultra indicatam summam, contractus vi caret, nisi beneplacitum apostolicum antecesserit; secus, requiritur et sufficit licentia, in scriptis data, Superioris ad normam constitutionum cum consensu sui Capituli seu Consilii per secreta suffragia manifestato; sed si agatur de monialibus aut sororibus iuris diocesani, accedat necesse est consensus, in scriptis praestitus, Ordinarii loci, necnon Superioris regularis, si monialium monasterium eidem subiectum sit."

§ 2. "In precibus pro obtinendo consensu ad contrahenda debita vel obligationes, exprimi debent alia debita vel obligationes, quibus ipsa persona moralis, religio vel provincia vel domus, ad eum diem gravatur; secus obtenta venia invalida est."

[72] § 1. "Res alienari minore pretio non debet quam quod in aestimatione indicatur."

§ 2. "Alienatio fiat per publicam licitationem aut saltem nota reddatur, nisi aliud circumstantiae suadeant; et res ei concedatur qui, omnibus perpensis, plus obtulerit."

§ 3. "Pecunia ex alienatione percepta caute, tuto et utiliter in commodum Ecclesiae collocetur."

and Question 102 inquires whether the necessary formalities for this alienation have been observed. Question 103 then asks:

> Did the institute, provinces or houses consume any stable or founded property or capital funds; for what reasons and by what authority.[73]

And Question 104 inquires:

> Are the general, provincial and local superiors and bursars making serious efforts to recover this property.

It is difficult to determine the precise meaning of these two questions. Questions 101 and 102 have already inquired into the legitimate alienation of property. Since it would be redundant to repeat the same enquiry, it seems that Question 103 refers to something other than legitimate alienation. Therefore, it must refer to illicit dissipation of fixed property. Question 104, then, would indicate that the Holy See wishes superiors to take steps to recover this property. An example of such an effort would be the institution of legal action to recover the property on the basis of the invalidity of alienation carried out without legitimate authorization.[74]

Closely allied to this question is Question 134, which reflects the mind of the Holy See that superiors take effective action to clear the institute, province or house of all responsibility for financial dealings carried out by individual religious who failed to observe the norms of the common or particular law.[75]

In regard to the investment of money, the List of Questions shows that a distinction is made between a permanent investment and a temporary one. The permanent investment of money means the disposition of it in such a manner as to assure its preservation for the future, at least in an equivalent form, or that it will pro-

[73] It seems that the question considers as synonymous the terms "stable or founded property or capital funds." The Latin is: "bona stabilia seu fundata et summas capitales." It is inconceivable that the Holy See would be inquiring here about the use of free "capital sums" for current expenses.

[74] Cf. can. 1530, § 1, 3o.

[75] Cf. can. 536, § 3: "Si contraxerit religiosus sine ulla superiorum licentia, ipsemet respondere debet, non autem religio vel provincia vel domus."

duce revenue (for example, the purchase of productive real estate, of stocks or bonds).[76] Question 119 inquires whether such investments have been made according to the prescriptions of the Code and the constitutions. The question makes reference to canon 533, which lists the circumstances in which the consent of the local ordinary is required for the investment of money.[77] Question 120 indicates that current funds not immediately needed for ordinary expenses should be invested on a temporary basis. The simplest manner in which to make such an investment is to deposit the money in a savings account, where it will draw a low rate of interest with the assurance that it can be withdrawn when it is needed.[78]

Authors do not agree whether a temporary investment is to be regulated by canon 533. Even before the publication of the List of Questions, the opinion which exempted such investments from the prescriptions of canon 533 was held to be probable and to reflect a norm which it was safe to follow.[79] The wording of Questions 119 and 120 gives even greater probability to this opinion. For Question 120 recommends a temporary investment of surplus funds, but makes no reference to canon 533. Question 119, however, when inquiring about permanent investments, does advert to the canon. In the context, therefore, Question 120 implies that temporary investments are *not* included in the purview of canon 533.

[76] Creusen-Ellis, *Religious Men and Women in Church Law*, p. 120, n. 156.

[77] Can. 533, § 1: "Pro pecuniae quoque collocatione servetur praescriptum can. 532, § 1; sed praevium consensum Ordinarii loci obtinere tenentur:

1º Antistita monialium et religionis iuris dioecesani pro cuiusvis pecuniae collocatione; imo, si monialium monasterium sit Superiori regulari subiectum, ipsius quoque consensus est necessarius;

2º Antistita in Congregatione religiosa iuris pontificii, si pecunia dotem professarum constituat, ad normam can. 549;

3º Superior vel Antistita domus Congregationis religiosae, si qui fundi domui tributi legative sint ad Dei cultum beneficentiamve eo ipso loco impendendam;

4º Religiosus quilibet, etsi Ordinis regularis alumnus, si pecunia data sit paroeciae vel missioni, aut religiosis intuitu paroeciae vel missionis."

[78] Schaefer, *De Religiosis*, p. 381, n. 714.

[79] Cf. Schaefer, *loc. cit.*

Section 6. Oblates

In the preamble of Chapter II of the List of Questions, enquiries are made concerning the various classes of persons in the community. In this context, Question 140 asks:

> Besides the persons who belong to the institute or society as members, by religious profession or lawful incorporation, are there others who are dedicated or given to it, or the like, without being members.

The next question inquires whether adequate provision is made for the spiritual life of these persons, and also for their material security. The persons mentioned here are commonly called "oblates," a term which has its historical roots in the Order of St. Benedict. In the early centuries of that order, it was a common practice that young boys be offered by their parents as candidates for the Benedictine life. They were known as "oblates" from the Latin "*oblatus*," which means "offered" or "given." When they grew older these candidates became professed members of the order.[80] However, the term came to have various meanings down through the centuries.[81] Oblates of the type described in Question 140 are not mentioned in the Code of Canon Law. But they are found in some religious institutes, for example, in the Order of Friars Minor.[82]

The regulations made for these members of the community in the Franciscan Order are reviewed here as examples of the desired provisions referred to in the List of Questions. In this

80 Brockhaus, *Religious Who Are Known as "Conversi"*, The Catholic University of America Canon Law Studies, No. 225 (Washington, D.C.: The Catholic University of America Press, 1946), pp. 2-3.

81 Cf. Almond, "Oblati, Oblatae, Oblates"— *The Catholic Encyclopedia*, XI, 188.

82 Cf. *Regula et Constitutiones Generales Ordinis Fratrum Minorum*, art. 24-33. In the former constitutions of the Friars Minor, the term "*oblati*" was used (cf. *Regula et Constitutiones Generales Fratrum Minorum* [Quaracchi: Ex Typographia Collegii S. Bonaventurae, 1922], art. 114); in the present constitutions the term has been dropped and these members are called "tertiaries."

order they must have the same qualifications as candidates for the lay brotherhood. [83] After a period spent as candidates, usually lasting six months, they are invested with a religious habit, which differs from that of the novices and from that of professed religious. [84] Following a year of probation, they profess the rule of the Third Order of St. Francis, making private vows of obedience and chastity. [85] Two years after the reception of the habit they may be designated as postulants for the novitiate, provided that they wish to enter the First Order. Those who do not enter the novitiate may be permitted to remain in the order as tertiaries. [86] From the moment of their reception of the tertiary habit they partake in all the indulgences and other spiritual privileges of the order, [87] and they must in all respects conform to the common life of the institute. [88] Finally, explicit provision is made for their education and spiritual formation. [89]

Section 7. The Postulancy and the Novitiate

In Article I of Chapter II, the List of Questions seeks information about the acceptance of candidates and about the training given to them during the postulancy and the novitiate. The subject matter of this section corresponds in a notable degree to the parallel section of the Code of Canon Law. [90] There are, however, a few points which indicate the mind of the Holy See on matters not mentioned in the Code.

Question 145 shows that, in schools for the training of candidates, the Holy See wishes young students to be kept separate from the older ones.

[83] *Ibid.*, art. 25.

[84] *Ibid.*, art. 26.

[85] *Ibid.*, art. 29; *Rituale Romano-Seraphicum Ordinis Fratrum Minorum* (3. ed., Romae: Schola Typographica "Pax et Bonum," 1955), Tit. V, Cap. II, n. 2 (p. 268).

[86] *Regula et Constitutiones Generales Ordinis Fratrum Minorum*, art. 32.

[87] *Ibid.*, art. 26, § 2.

[88] *Ibid.*, art. 33.

[89] *Ibid.*, art. 28; art. 31.

[90] I. e., cc. 538-571.

In regard to the discipline of the novitiate, Question 159 refers to canon 554, § 3, which directs superiors to assign to the novitiate house only those religious who offer a praiseworthy example of regular observance. The question adds a logical corollary, namely, that religious who are not exemplary should not be permitted to remain there.

Question 164 concerns the expenses incurred for food and clothing with reference to postulants and novices. Canon 570, § 1, permits superiors to seek reimbursement for these expenses, in an amount specified by the constitutions or by formal agreement. While it leaves this right intact, Question 164 nevertheless labels it a serious abuse to delay profession on the score that such expenses have not been paid.

Question 180 refers to the making of a will as required of novices in congregations by canon 569, § 3. The question reads:

> a) Did novices of a congregation, before their first profession of temporary vows, freely make a will in due form, valid according to the civil law, regarding their present or future property (c. 569, § 3).
>
> b) Did they afterwards render this will valid according to the civil law (c. 569, § 3).

It can be inferred from the wording of this question that, if a novice is not old enough before profession to make a will valid in civil law, he should nevertheless make the will and, when he comes of age, he should remake the will. This conclusion is supported by Question 182, which asks: "Are the aforesaid documents a), b) faithfully kept in the archives ?" It is thus implied that there may be two such documents, one made before the novice was of legal age, and the other drawn up after reached his majority.

It is now the mind of the Sacred Congregation of Religious that, except for wills in favor of pious causes, the will mentioned in canon 569, § 3, signifies that will alone which is *valid* in civil law. Hence, only a civilly valid will need be made, unless it is a question of matter governed by canon 1513.[91] Moreover, a will which has been invalidly made may now be changed after profession apart from any specific permission of the Holy See. Hence, there is now no need for the two documents referred to in Question 182, except in the case of the wills mentioned by canon 1513.[92]

Section 8. Religious Who Leave the Institute

Question 197 considers the departure from religious life on the part of a woman religious who has been received without a dowry, or with a very small dowry. In this case, if the religious leaves the institute, there will be no dowry to be returned to her, or at best a small one. The Code provides that, if the departing religious has been received without a dowry, she shall be given an appropriate charitable assistance in the event that she is unable to provide for herself.[93] In the Code there is no mention of assistance to be given to one who has been received with only a small dowry. But Question 197 asks if such assistance is also extended when the dowry itself is insufficient to provide for the needs of the departing religious.[94]

In a later section of the List of Questions the rights of religious who are dismissed from the institute are considered, and certain elements not clearly specified in the Code of Canon Law are added.

91 Canon 1513: § 1. "Qui ex iure naturae et ecclesiastico libere valet de suis bonis statuere, potest ad causas pias, sive per actum inter vivos sive per actum mortis causa, bona relinquere."

§ 2. "In ultimis voluntatibus in bonum Ecclesiae serventur, si fieri possit, sollemnitates iuris civilis; hae si omissae fuerint, heredes moneantur ut testatoris voluntatem adimpleant."

92 Cf. the private reply of the Sacred Congregation of Religious, March 26, 1957, reported in *CLD, Annual Supplement through 1960*, under canon 569, and in *CpRM*, XXXVII (1958), 56-68, with commentary by Gutiérrez. Gutiérrez points out that this reply, though private, is virtually general, since it expresses the practice of the Sacred Congregation of Religious for all such cases. — *Ibid.*, pp. 59-60.

93 Can. 643, § 2.

94 Question 197 reflects an earlier declaration of the Sacred Congregation of Religious. Cf "Dubium," 2 mart. 1924 — *AAS*, XVI (1924), 165.

The Code enacts certain requirements to safeguard the rights of dismissed religious. Thus, canon 647, § 2, 4°, allows religious dismissed in temporary vows to have recourse to the Holy See against the act of dismissal, while canons 652 and 666 require ratification by the Holy See for decrees or sentences of dismissal for perpetually professed religious. These points are qualified by Question 253, which makes it clear that, until a response is given to the appeal, or until the confirmation of the decree or sentence, the religious should not be forced to leave the institute.

Question 254 refers to dismissed religious who are still bound by the obligations of the vows. A religious in perpetual vows is not usually released from his vows through dismissal from the institute, unless such a release is effected in virtue of the constitutions or by apostolic indult. [95] When subjects are still bound by the vows, Question 254 indicates that superiors should "show solicitude regarding their condition." In other words, the community should not display an utter disregard for such religious, since they are obliged to return to religious life, and the institute is bound to receive them when they have given proof of amendment. [96] Question 254 implies that superiors should seek to foster the return of these religious, and to encourage them in their efforts to prove themselves worthy to be reinstated.

Question 260 indicates that superiors should be solicitous also for exclaustrated religious. They must, if it seems necessary, renew the indult which will allow them to live outside the cloister. Moreover, they should try to ensure that the exclaustrated religious lives a worthy religious life, and returns to the institute as soon as possible. Question 261 urges that a similar solicitude be shown towards clerical religious who are on probation in a diocese with a view to secularization.

Section 9. Care of the Sick

Questions 211-213 imply certain obligations on the part of superiors in respect to the care of the sick. There is no legislation

[95] Can. 669, § 1.

[96] Can. 672, § 1.

in the Code on this point, although it is one of the corollaries of the common life required of religious that superiors provide for their temporal needs.[97] It is left to the constitutions of the institute to specify the obligations of superiors in this matter. In addition, this section of the List of Questions points out that sick and aged religious should be cared for with special charity. Within the limits of religious poverty, they should lack nothing necessary for the recovery of their health and for their spiritual consolation. If they must be cared for outside the religious house, they should be visited frequently. It is suggested that the institute have a special house for the care of its sick and aged members.

Section 10. Religious Modesty

Question 214-222 concern themselves with matters pertaining to the vow of chastity. Some of the points covered were previously considered in the *Normae* of 1901, such as the assignment of a companion to sisters visiting in the parlor, the careful locking of the convent door at night, and the complete separation of the chaplain's quarters from the part of the convent reserved for the sisters.[98] Over and beyond these points, the following obligations of superiors are indicated by the List of Questions:

1) that of vigilance and supervision over the reading matter of subjects;[99]

2) that of supervision over the use of the telephone and of the radio;[100]

3) that of punishing religious who have been guilty of offenses against chastity with students entrusted to their care;[101]

[97] Can. 594.

[98] Cf. *Normae*, nn. 175-179.

[99] *Elenchus Quaestionum*, q. 214, c).

[100] *Ibid.*, q. 214, d). Cf. also the letter of the Sacred Congregation of Religious to general superiors, regarding the use of radio and television, August 6, 1957. This letter is not published in *AAS*, but it is found in translation in *CLD*, IV, 206-209.

[101] *Ibid.*, q. 216.

and, 4) that of arranging the parlors in such a way that the persons conversing in them can be seen by persons outside the parlor.[102]

Question 221 refers to the prescription of canon 607, which imposes upon superioresses and local ordinaries the duty of making sure that sisters do not leave the convent without a companion. The canon makes this exception, that in cases of necessity a companion is not required. The wording of Question 221 broadens this exception, in two respects: (1) it adds the word "prudent" to "necessity," thus implying that one should not be unreasonably strict in interpreting this prescription of the canon, and (2) it states that a companion should be assigned "especially for the purpose of making a visit," implying that the prudent necessity which justifies the omission of a companion is more easily verified on other occasions.

Section 11. Religious in Military Service

Questions 269-274 refer to religious who have been called into military service. The status of these religious is not regulated by the Code, for such military service is imposed by civil authority in disregard of the privilege of clerical immunity.[103] Prior to the Code the Holy See published a decree which established norms for the conduct of these religious, provided for their supervision, and defined the status of their religious profession.[104] This legislation retained its force even after the promulgation of the Code,[105] until the year 1957, when it was superseded by a new decree, which reconsidered the entire subject.[106] According to this decree, no religious may make final profession until he has finished his compulsory military service, or has been declared exempt from it.

102 *Ibid.*, q. 219, a).

103 Cf. cc. 121, 614.

104 S. Cong. de Rel., decr. *Inter reliquas*, 11 ian. 1911 — *AAS*, III (1911), 37-39.

105 S. Cong. de Rel., 15 iul. 1919 — *AAS*, XI (1919), 321.

106 S. Cong. de Rel., decr. *Militare servitium*, 30 iul. 1957 — *AAS*, XLIX (1957), 871-874.

While he is in service, his vows are suspended, unless his major superior has made an exception in this regard. The decree also outlines the procedure required for the departure of the religious from the institute or for his dismissal. Further, it determines the ownership of property which may be received by the religious while in military service. The List of Questions adds to the matter of the decree by indicating that superiors should frequently communicate with their subjects in service, and that they must watch over their conduct and employ means designed to ensure their perseverance in the religious life.

Section 12. Works of the Apostolate

Chapter III of the List of Questions refers to various types of apostolic activity engaged in by religious. The areas covered by the questions include missionary activity, the administration of parishes, educational endeavors, the practice of the corporal works of mercy, the apostolate of the press, and the promotion of Catholic Action. In keeping with the scope of the present article, reference is made here only to those questions which indicate the mind of the Holy See in matters not already treated by the Code of Canon Law.

In reference to the apostolate of teaching, Question 301 asks:

> Are there schools which are attended by both sexes; as regards fixing the age beyond which boys may not be admitted or retained, have the prescriptions made by the Ordinaries been observed.

Since the promulgation of the List of Questions, however, there is a possibility that further information may be required on this point. On December 8, 1957, an instruction on coeducation was issued by the Sacred Congregation of Religious. [107] The instruction

[107] "De iuvenum utriusque sexus promiscua institutione," *AAS*, L (1958), 99-103. Though emanating from the Sacred Congregation of Religious, this Instruction resulted from a joint meeting of members of the Sacred Consistorial Congregation, the Congregation for the Oriental Church, the Congregation of the Council,

reaffirmed the Holy See's opposition to coeducation in secondary schools,[108] and recommended that "coinstitutional" schools be had wherein certain facilities can be used by boys and girls at different times. If this arrangement cannot be made, the Instruction directs that in the quinquennial reports a number of questions be inserted, in order to inform the Holy See of the manner of directing such schools.[109] In the future, then, the quinquennial report must include an account of the manner of carrying out coeducation in secondary schools, in regard to its organization as well as its effects.[110]

Also in reference to the apostolate of teaching, Question 302 emphasizes the strict obligation of superiors to ensure the scientific, pedagogic and spiritual training of rectors, prefects, and teachers employed in schools conducted by religious.[111] Allied to this question is Question 308, which indicates that religious who are engaged in the corporal works of mercy—for example, nursing, social work, the care of orphans—must receive competent training for these tasks. It is recommended that they earn diplomas or degrees which are recognized by the civil authorities. In addition they should receive practical training in the work, under the supervision of more experienced religious.

Finally, it is indicated by Question 316 that the Holy See wishes religious "to promote Catholic Action and to collaborate

---

the Congregation for the Propagation of the Faith, and the Congregation for Universities and Seminaries. And Pope Pius XII commanded that it be observed not only by religious but also by others to whom the supervision of the education of youth is entrusted.

108 Cf. Pius XI, litt. encyc. *Divini illius Magistri*, 31 dec. 1929 — *AAS*, XXII (1930), 72.

109 "Quodsi eiusmodi 'coinstitutio' haberi non possit, praecipitur ut in relationes quinquennales opportunus numerus quaestionum inducatur, quibus Sedes Apostolica certior reddatur de agendi modo in scholis, ubi utriusque sexus iuvenes promiscue educantur." — *AAS*, L (1958), 101.

110 Cf. Frison, "Adnotationes," *CpRM*, XXXVII (1958), 279-280. Cf. also Huot, "Adnotationes," *Monitor Ecclesiasticus*, LXXXIII (1958), 241-247.

111 Art. 30 of the *Stat. Gen.* requires the proper preparation of teachers in the seminaries of religious.

in it." Although this subject is not mentioned in the Code, Pope Pius XI urged the superiors general of religious institutes to promote Catholic Action and to foster an apostolic spirit in youth, especially by means of an education duly adapted to that end.[112]

[112] Cf. the letter of the Cardinal Secretary of State (Eugenio Pacelli), March 15, 1936. This letter is not published in the *AAS*, but can be found in translation in *CLD*, II, 65-67.

CHAPTER VI

THE QUINQUENNIAL REPORT AS AN INSTRUMENT OF SUPERVISION BY RELIGIOUS SUPERIORS

The decree *Cum transactis* binds the superiors who make the quinquennial report to answer the questions sincerely, completely, intelligently and conscientiously. [1] To ensure that the report measures up to this standard, it must be submitted to both the personal and collective scrutiny of the members of the supreme council. [2] If a councillor conscientiously feels that the report is deficient he may communicate his objections directly to the Sacred Congregation of Religious. Indeed, he may be bound in conscience to do so if the case calls for it. [3]

It is an arduous and demanding task for superiors to gather the information necessary for the report. For a large order or congregation this may seem to be too demanding an assignment. Nevertheless it is the opinion of the writer that an accurate answer to the questions is not beyond the realm of practical possibility for all institutes. Moreover, the effort to acquire the needed information is rewarding, since it furnishes higher superiors with a valuable instrument of supervision. As Pope Pius XII reminded superiors general of religious orders and congregations of men, it is the duty of superiors to lead their subjects securely to eternal life, with clear vision, with firm leadership and, if necessary, with a strong hand. He admonished them never to forget that God will demand an accounting not only for themselves as individuals, but also for all the subjects over whom they have been in charge. He added that, for the attainment of Gospel perfection, religious

1 *Cum transactis*, n. VI. Cf. *supra*, p. 50.

2 *Cum transactis*, n. VII. The constitutions of the institute determine the membership of this council.

3 *Cum transactis*, n. VIII.

discipline and observance are necessary, especially in view of the weakness of human nature. Superiors were advised never to relax their vigilance, but to apply their guidance both to the regular life within the community and to the entire apostolic work of the institute. Such guidance, he observed, is not always welcome to "human nature, inclined as it is to laxity." [4]

The very fact that the questionnaire for the quinquennial report is so detailed affords superiors general an opportunity to exercise the supervision demanded by their office, and this in a manner which may be more acceptable to some subjects. The while they are rightly seeking the information necessary for the quinquennial report, superiors can exercise their duty of vigilance over the institute.

Moreover, experience has shown that an evaluating checklist, such as that which the List of Questions provides, is useful to the degree that it is specific. The questionnaire is valuable to superiors as a means of recalling to their minds the basic principles which should guide them in the government of the community. They may not enjoy compiling these reports, but if these are properly executed they can serve as a valuable self-evaluation for the local, provincial and general administrations. [5]

Finally, the necessity of gathering the detailed information required by the quinquennial report can effectively serve to foster zeal for a more perfect religious life among the members of the institute. [6] The following paragraphs will offer a method whereby these benefits may be attained through a conscientious approach to the quinquennial report. The method suggested here is given only by way of example. In presenting it the writer has in mind

[4] Cf. Pius XII, allocutio, 11 febr. 1958 — *AAS*, L (1958), 153-161.

[5] Cf. Frison, "The Laws of Training in the Apostolic Constitution *Sedes Sapientiae*," — *The Jurist*, XXI (1961), 377.

[6] "Quae quidem omnia, etsi minutissima, haud spernenda vel levia habenda sunt, cum perfectae vitae religiosae, zelo apostolatus decoratae, apprime respondent religiosamque perfectionem aemulatione ac desiderio suscitent." — Pugliese, "Adnotationes de Quinquennali Relatione a Religionibus, a Societatibus Vitae Communis et ab Institutis Saecularibus Facienda," in *Monitor Ecclesiasticus*, LXXV (1950), 195-196.

a large centralized institute divided into many provinces. Adaptations of it could easily be made in accordance with the nature and individual characteristics of the various institutes.

The method is based upon a system of reports to be sent in to the general curia by every house and province. Each year a series of questionnaires would be distributed by the motherhouse to the provincial headquarters, and a second series to the individual houses. Annually each province would be required to submit statistical reports covering the members and the houses of the province, and the apostolic works carried on by them. The provincial reports would be based on corresponding reports submitted by the individual houses to the provincial superior.

Of greater import would be a disciplinary report submitted to the general curia annually by each province. The form for this report should be based on the List of Questions for the quinquennial report to the Holy See. It should be so designed that it covers all the information the general headquarters needs to obtain from the provinces in order to fill out the quinquennial report accurately. In addition, each house would be required to send *directly to the motherhouse* an annual report, similarly based on appropriate questions selected from the List of Questions for the quinquennial report. Finally, every five years the provincial procurator would be required to furnish all the specified financial information necessary for the quinquennial report.

In this way the motherhouse would be able to fulfill accurately the requirement that the "replies given to the questions proposed must always be sincere and as far as possible complete and based on careful inquiry." [7] And this could well obtain despite a large number of religious and houses. Two other elements of this system would have an equally great effect upon religious discipline. In the first place, the questions to be answered by provincial and local superiors would call to their attention the various obligations of the religious life, and form an outline, as it were, of what the institute and the Holy See expect of them and their communities in regard to religious discipline. Secondly, each community could

[7] *Cum transactis,* n. VI.

be required to discuss the report before it is submitted. It would thus have the yearly advantage of a self-evaluation embracing the obligations of the religious life and religious spirit. [8]

Undoubtedly, for the officials involved, the obligation of organizing the quinquennial report will always remain a demanding task. For the institute, however, the quinquennial report can become an effective means of supervision over religious discipline. Furthermore, it is an effective instrument to acquaint superiors with the obligations of their office. Finally, it affords the community the opportunity to re-assess its dedication to the sincere pursuit of religious perfection.

[8] The method here suggested is based upon the system worked out by the Religious Sisters of Mercy of the Union in the United States of America, whose motherhouse is in Bethesda, Maryland. A description of their system, along with copies of the various forms used by the institute, was graciously supplied to the writer by Very Reverend Mother Mary Regina, R.S.M., Mother General.

CHAPTER VII

THE ROLE OF THE LOCAL ORDINARY IN RELATION TO THE QUINQUENNIAL REPORT

According to the Code of Canon Law, only the superioresses general of religious institutes of pontifical approval are required to obtain the signature of the local ordinary upon the quinquennial report. The local ordinary referred to in the law is the one in whose diocese the superioress general and her council reside. [1]

It should be recalled here that, according to the Code and the Instruction which formerly governed the quinquennial report, [2] the classes of institutes obliged to send in a report were fewer than those required to do so under the present regulations. [3] Because of this difference, there are now several distinctions to be made in regard to the necessity for the signature of the local ordinary.

Among the superiors of institutes of men, those who are *not* required to obtain the signature of the local ordinary are: the abbot primate; the abbot superior of a monastic congregation; and, if it be of pontifical approval, the superior general of any religious institute, society of the common life without public vows, or secular institute; finally, the president of any federation of houses of religious institutes, societies of the common life, or secular institutes. [4]

In regard to women religious, the only reports for which the signature of the local ordinary is *not* required are those of major

[1] Can. 510.

[2] S. Cong. de Rel., decr. *Sancitum est*, 8 mart. 1922 — *AAS*, XIV (1922), 161-163. Cf. *supra*, pp. 35-38.

[3] Cf. *supra*, pp. 40-41.

[4] This enumeration is based on can. 510 and the decree *Cum transactis*, in as far as all those who are mentioned must send the Holy See a report, but receive no mention either in the canon or in the decree, among those for whose report the signature of the local ordinary is required.

superioresses of monasteries of nuns subject to a regular superior. For these monasteries, the regular superior is directed to add to the report any remarks he may see fit to make. He is then to sign it and send it to the Sacred Congregation within the year in which the report is to be made. [5]

For the reports of all other categories of institutes, houses, or federations, the signature of the local ordinary is required. Further distinctions, however, must also be made in regard to these groups.

Some reports of women religious need merely be signed by the ordinary; it is the superior herself who sends these to the Sacred Congregation. To this category belong the reports of religious institutes, of societies of the common life, of secular institutes, and of federations, provided all of these be of pontifical approval. [6]

Other reports must be signed by the local ordinary, who is directed to add such remarks as he may see fit, and to send them to the Sacred Congregation himself. To this category belong the following reports:

1) the reports of major superiors of independent monasteries of men, which belong neither to a monastic congregation nor to a federation of independent monasteries; [7]

2) the reports of superioresses of monasteries of nuns who are not subject to regular superiors; [8]

3) the reports of independent and autonomous religious houses, or of independent and autonomous houses of a society without vows, or of a secular institute, provided such houses are not united in a federation. [9]

A third category consists of reports of diocesan institutes, whether these be congregations, societies of the common life, or

[5] *Cum transactis*, n. IV, 2º.

[6] *Cum transactis*, n. VII.

[7] *Ibid.*, n. IV, 1º.

[8] *Ibid.*, n. IV, 2º.

[9] *Ibid.*, n. IV, 4º. Such houses could be houses of men or women, and of diocesan approval or of pontifical approval. They differ from those which receive mention in n. IV, 1º and 2º, in that the first mentioned are *monasteries* whereas the houses mentioned in 4º are non-monastic.

secular institutes. The local ordinary where the principal house is located must communicate these reports to the local ordinaries where other houses of the institute may be established. Then he shall sign the report, add his own judgment and that of the other ordinaries regarding the congregation, society, or secular institute in question, and shall, within the year, send the report to the Sacred Congregation.[10]

From the foregoing data it will be noted that, for women's institutes or federations of pontifical approval, the local ordinary merely signs the report, while the general superior herself sends it to the Sacred Congregation. But for all of the houses or institutes mentioned in n. IV, 1°-4°[11] (with the exception of monasteries of nuns subject to regulars), the local ordinary signs the report, adds his own comments, and sends it to Sacred Congregation himself.

This difference of procedure presents a juridical problem, which one can perhaps best explore by considering what is intended when to the signature of the local ordinary is required. In regard to the quinquennial report of pontifical congregations of women religious, the primary duty of the local ordinary is to authenticate the document. That this was the purpose of this signature in the pre-Code jurisprudence is clear from the *Normae* of 1901. The *Normae* directed the local ordinary to "authenticate with his signature" the triennal report which was then required.[12] There is no reason to change this directive today. Moreover, the Holy See is not wont to deal directly with institutes of women religious, but prefers to deal with them through one of the organs of the hierarchy. By his signature the local ordinary testifies that the report was drawn up and signed by the superioress general and the members of her council, as is prescribed in the law. He does not vouch for

10 *Ibid.*, n. IV, 3°.

11 These houses or institutes are: independent monasteries of men; monasteries of women; diocesan congregations, societies, or secular institutes; independent and autonomous houses, whether they pertain to institutes of religious or to societies without vows, or to secular institutes.

12 "Cui relationi Ordinarius domus principalis, nomen suum apponendo, fidem faciat." — *Normae*, art. 262.

the contents of the report; he vouches only for its authenticity. [13]

Larraona holds that the ordinary has no authority to investigate whether the facts reported by the religious are true. [14] He argues that, if the ordinary were empowered to survey and pass judgment on the contents of the report, then the whole government, discipline, and temporal administration of congregations would be brought under the judgment, vigilance, examination, and, as it were, under a certain visitation of the ordinary. But these areas are withdrawn from the authority and vigilance of the ordinary by canon 618, § 2, 2°. [15]

The present writer cannot agree completely with this reasoning of Larraona. Undoubtedly, canon 510, in requiring the signature of the local ordinary for the quinquennial report, does not intend to subject to the ordinary the whole government, discipline, and temporal administration of pontifical congregations of women. And the reason given by Larraona is valid, as far as it goes. That is, canon 618, § 2, 2°, forbids the local ordinary to interfere in the internal government and discipline of institutes approved by the Holy See. But the canon adds, "except for cases expressed

[13] Cf. Larraona, "Commentarium Codicis,"— *CpR*, VIII (1927), 282-283; Schaefer, *De Religiosis*, p. 270, n. 541; Farrell, *The Rights and Duties of the Local Ordinary Regarding Congregations of Women Religious of Pontifical Approval*, The Catholic University of America Canon Law Studies, No. 128 (Washington, D. C.: The Catholic University of America Press, 1941), p. 90; Ellis, "Quinquennial Report, 1951,"— *Review for Religious*, X (1951), 22; Pugliese, "Adnotationes de Quinquennali Relatione a Religionibus, a Societatibus Vitae Communis et ab Institutis Saecularibus Facienda," — *Monitor Ecclesiasticus*, LXXV (1950), 190-191.

[14] "Ordinarius non respondet nisi de forma; sua subscriptione testatur ipsum confectum esse et signatum a Superiorissa Generali et eius Consiliariis, prout in iure praescriptum est. Ceterum Ordinarius non debet, neque potest, investigare an illa vera sint quae allegantur."— *loc. cit.*

[15] Can. 618, § 2, 2°. "[In religionibus tamen iuris pontificii Ordinario loci non licet:] Sese ingerere in regimen internum ac disciplinam, exceptis casibus in iure expressis; nihilominus in religionibus laicalibus ipse potest ac debet inquirere num disciplina ad constitutionum normam vigeat, num quid sana doctrina morumve probitas detrimenti ceperit, num contra clausuram peccatum sit, num Sacramenta aequa stataque frequentia suscipiantur... "

in the law." It is this exception that Larraona ignores in his argument. What is more, the canon itself states such an exception, when it continues:

> Nevertheless, in regard to lay institutes, the local ordinary can and must enquire: whether the discipline is maintained conformably to the constitutions, whether sound doctrine and good morals have suffered in any way, whether there have been breaches of the law of enclosure, whether the reception of the sacraments is regular and frequent. [16]

In view of this prescription, it should be concluded that the ordinary would not be overstepping his competence if, in addition to authenticating the report with his signature, he studied the report in regard to the points committed to his vigilance by canon 618.

The foregoing considerations look simply to the quinquennial reports of pontifical institutes of women religious. It was for these reports only that canon 510 required the signature of the local ordinary. The same line of reasoning may not be used in regard to those institutes or houses whose obligation to submit a report rests only upon the decree *Cum transactis*. As has been noted, to these reports the local ordinary is instructed to add comments together with his signature. It cannot be valid, then, to say that the local ordinary merely authenticates them. Pugliese presents two arguments in an attempt to justify the requirement that the local ordinary add his comments to these reports, and that he, and not the religious superior, forward them to the Holy See. In the first argument he states that the required comments are justified by the fact that the religious upon whose reports the local ordinary is to comment are fully subject to him. [17] In his second argument Pugliese appeals to canon 512, § 1, 1° and § 2, 1°. [18] He reasons that since this canon obliges the local ordi-

[16] Quoted from *Canonical Legislation concerning Religious: Authorized English Translation* (Westminster, Maryland: The Newman Press, 1948), p. 51.

[17] "Agitur enim de Religiosis plene Ordinario loci subiectis." — Pugliese, *ibid.*, p. 192.

[18] Can. 512: § 1. "Ordinarius loci per se vel per alium quinto quoque anno visitare debet:

nary to conduct the visitation of monasteries, it is fitting that the quinquennial report of independent monasteries and houses be sent through the same ordinary. [19]

In these remarks Pugliese ignores the jurisprudential problem raised by the decree *Cum transactis*; indeed, he even begs the question. For among the reports upon which the local ordinary comments and which he sends to Rome are those of exempt monasteries of men, [20] and of independent houses of pontifical approval. [21] It is entirely incorrect to say that these houses are "fully subject to the local ordinary." The limitations the law places upon the supervision of the local ordinary in regard to pontifical institutes [22] provide sufficient proof of the incongruity of this statement. *A fortiori*, the exempt monasteries involved are not "fully subject to the local ordinary." Nor can a valid appeal be made to the local ordinary's right of visitation in order to explain his role in regard to the reports under consideration. For canon 512, in § 1, 1° and § 2, 1°, cited by Pugliese, directs the local ordinary to visit the monasteries of nuns. The same canon, in a number not cited by Pugliese, directs the local ordinary to visit the institutes of diocesan approval. [23] He is also to visit clerical congregations of pontifical approval, even if they are exempt, but the scope of his visitation in these houses is severely limited. [24] In regard to lay institutes

---

1°. Singula monialium monasteria quae sibi vel Sedi Apostolicae immediate subiecta sunt... "

§ 2. "Visitare quoque eodem tempore debet:

1°. Monasteria monialium, quae regularibus subduntur, circa ea quae ad clausurae legem spectant; imo etiam circa alia omnia, si Superior regularis ea a quinque annis non visitaverit."

19 "Cum autem in can. 512, § 1, 1° et § 2, 1°, obligatio imponitur Ordinario locorum quinto quoque anno singula Monasteria canonice visitandi, opportune statutum est in Decreto *Cum transactis* ut Relatio, quam Monasteria huiusmodi et Domus sui iuris independentes conficere quoque debent... ad Ordinarios transmittatur et per Ordinarios eiusdem exemplar ad S. C. de Religiosis perveniat."— *Ibid.*, p. 197.

20 *Cum transactis*, n. IV, 1°.

21 *Ibid.*, n. IV, 4°.

22 Cf. can. 618.

23 Can. 512, § 1, 2°.

24 Can. 512, § 2, 2°: "[Visitare quoque eodem tempore debet:] Singulas domos Congregationis clericalis iuris pontificii etiam exemptae, in iis quae per-

of pontifical approval, the local ordinary's rights of visitation are limited by the provisions of canon 618.[25] Canon 512, then, whether in the sections cited by Pugliese or in the sections not cited by him, does not serve to explain the local ordinary's role in regard to the reports of exempt monasteries of men and of independent houses of pontifical institutes of men.

The problem still remains, then, to explain this anomaly: the reports of some pontifical — and even exempt — institutes of men are subjected to the comments of the local ordinary, but the reports of pontifical congregations of women are not subject to his comments. Why?

It could perhaps be argued that for independent houses the observations of the ordinary concern not the report, but the religious themselves. In other words, it would be a judgment about the house, based not on the report, but on other, independent, observations. Such an interpretation would indeed mean that the ordinary would do no violence to canon 618, § 2. Nor would his actions contravene the exemption of certain of the religious houses concerned. But such an interpretation does not fit the text and context of the pertinent paragraphs of the decree *Cum transactis*.[26] It is true that these paragraphs do not explicitly specify the object of the ordinary's remarks or observations.[27] Nevertheless, in the context it seems that they must refer to the report itself. So clear is this inference that, if any other interpretation were intended, a very definite indication of it would undoubtedly have been made.[28]

---

tinent ad ecclesiam, sacrarium, oratorium publicum, sedem ad sacramentum poenitentiae."

[25] Can. 512, § 2, 3º: "[Visitare quoque eodem tempore debet:] Singulas domos Congregationis laicalis iuris pontificii non solum in iis, de quibus in superiore numero, sed etiam in aliis, quae ad internam disciplinam spectant, ad normam tamen can. 618, § 2, n. 2."

[26] N. IV, 1º and 4º. The text is to be found *supra*, pp. 40–41.

[27] An ablative absolute is used in the Latin: "propriis, si casus ferat, additis animadversionibus."

[28] In fact, for diocesan institutes such a distinction is made, when it is stated that the ordinary or ordinaries concerned should make a judgment on both the

The other possible explanation of the anomaly in question is to recognize it as a juridical fact, and to seek reasons why the Holy See would make such an arrangement. This solution puts the following interpretation on the directives of the decree *Cum transactis*: it is clear that independent monasteries and houses, even though they be of pontifical right and, in some cases, exempt, are to submit their quinquennial report to the local ordinary. The latter is to add any remarks he may see fit to make about the report itself, and then he is to send a copy of the report to the Sacred Congregation of Religious. Such an interpretation seems the only acceptable one.

In the search for reasons why the Holy See has made such an arrangement, no help is supplied by the canonical authors. However, this one salient fact stands out: the only institutes of pontifical approval whose reports are subject to the comments of the local ordinary are *independent* houses. [29] It seems accordingly that these reports are to be submitted to the judgment of the local ordinary precisely because they are reports of independent houses. This requirement is quite in line with the contemporary practice of the Holy See which encourages independent houses to become federated. [30]

---

report *and* the institute: "Ordinarius loci domus principis curare debet: a) Ut exemplar Relationis etiam cum aliis Ordinariis in quorum Dioecesibus domus Congregationis vel Societatis existunt, communicetur; qui Ordinarii, Relatione attente examinata, animadversiones quas opportunas iudicaverint atque proprium iudicium circa Congregationem, scripto communicent cum Ordinario domus principis vel directo transmittant Sacrae Congregationi de Religiosis." — Sacra Congregatio de Religiosis, *Elenchus Quaestionum pro Congregationibus et Societatibus Iuris Dioecesani* (Typis Polyglottis Vaticanis, 1957), "Animadvertenda," B), 6, a), pp. 3-4.

29 Other monasteries or houses which are *sui iuris* but which belong to a monastic congregation or to a federation are not subject in this way to the local ordinary. For them the head of the congregation or federation sends a report to Rome. If they are federations of *women's* institutes, the local ordinary does indeed sign it, but adds no comment. Cf. *supra*, pp. 81-82.

30 Cf. for example, the General Statutes for nuns contained in *Sponsa Christi*, art. VII, § 2 — *AAS*, XLIII (1951), 18; S. Cong. de Rel., instr. 23 nov. 1950, art. XVII — *AAS*, XLIII (1951), 41.

It must be admitted that, in this instance, the decree *Cum transactis* does some violence to canon 618. For it requires a pontifically approved institute to submit to the examination and judgment of the local ordinary the items of the quinquennial report concerning its government, discipline, and temporal administration. *A fortiori*, some violence is done to the exemption enjoyed by some of the monasteries concerned. Nevertheless, it should be recalled that a primary purpose of the privilege of exemption is the conservation and promotion of the unity of a religious institute which, extended to several dioceses, would, without exemption, be governed by several different ordinaries. [31] Therefore, it does not violate the *spirit* of exemption, considered in the light of its purpose, that the report of entirely independent houses should be subjected to the scrutiny of the local ordinary. This conclusion should not be broadened to mean that the local ordinary is thereby given further supervisory jurisdiction over such houses. He is authorized merely to communicate to the Sacred Congregation his comments upon the reports submitted to him.

The procedure prescribed by canon 510 has not been changed for pontifical congregations of women religious, nor for women's societies of the common life which are of pontifical approval. And the same procedure has been applied to reports of superioresses general of secular institutes of pontifical approval and to federations of independent houses. [32] For these groups, then, the interpretation common among authors who wrote before the appearance of the decree *Cum transactis* is still valid, namely, that the function of the signature of the local ordinary is merely to authenticate the report.

[31] Cf. Schaefer, *De Religiosis*, p. 760, n. 1275.

[32] *Cum transactis*, n. VII.

CHAPTER VIII

THE QUINQUENNIAL REPORT AS A BASIS FOR DOCTRINAL INTERPRETATION

The List of Questions for the quinquennial report is not intended to be an official commentary on the law governing religious. Nor can it be considered to be an authentic interpretation of this law. Authentic interpretation is that explanation of the meaning of a law which is made by the legislator, or by one to whom the legislator has granted this power. [1] For interpretation to be termed authentic the interpreter must also, of set purpose, intend to determine the sense of the law and to make the acceptance of its meaning obligatory. [2] Pope Benedict XV limited the power to make general authentic interpretations of the Code of Canon Law to the Pontifical Commission for the Authentic Interpretation of the Canons of the Code. [3] Therefore it is evident that the *Elenchus Quaestionum* for the quinquennial report is not a vehicle of authentic interpretation of the Code.

The List of Questions can and does serve, however, as a source of doctrinal interpretation, since the Sacred Congregation has, in practice, adopted one or the other opinion on certain disputed points. While this does not constitute authentic interpretation, it does

[1] Vermeersch-Creusen, *Epitome Iuris Canonici* (7. ed., 3 vols., Mechliniae-Romae: H. Dessain, 1949-1956), I, p. 118, n. 120 (hereafter cited *Epitome*). Cf. can. 17, § 1: "Leges authentice interpretatur legislator eiusve successor et is cui potestas interpretandi fuerit ab eisdem commissa."

[2] Michiels, *Normae Generales*, I, 483-484.

[3] "Exemplum decessorum Nostrorum secuti, qui decretorum Concilii Tridentini interpretationem proprio Patrum Cardinalium coetui commiserunt, Consilium seu *Commissionem*, uti vocant, constituimus, cui uni ius erit Codicis authentice interpretandi, audita tamen, in rebus maioris momenti, Sacra ea Congregatione cuius propria res sit, quae Consilio disceptanda proponitur."—Motu propr., *Cum iuris canonici*, 15 sept. 1917, in *AAS*, IX (1917), 483.

show the mind of the Holy See in regard to the meaning of the laws in question. Thus the interpretation afforded by the wording of some of the questions can be considered to be of greater value than that of a merely private doctrinal interpretation, which has been defined as that "given by private persons skilled in canon law." [4] For "the Congregations apply the canons to current questions, and this application of the law is its practical interpretation; it is also official, in the sense that it comes from lawful authority." [5]

This chapter considers several canons which have been given various interpretations by authors. The interpretations of the authors will be noted, followed by the interpretation based upon certain questions of the *Elenchus Quaestionum*. While this interpretation does not constitute authentic interpretation of the canons, it does reflect the meaning put upon them by the Sacred Congregation of Religious at the time the *Elenchus* was composed.

Article I. Catechetical Instruction

According to canon 509, § 2, 2°, *conversi* and *familiares* should receive instructions in Christian doctrine at least twice a month. In addition, a pious exhortation should be addressed to all members of a religious house, especially in a lay institute. [6] Authors do not agree on the meaning of the word "*familiares*" in canon 509. Their definitions of this term fall into two general categories. One opinion holds that the word extends to all those who dwell in a religious house day and night, by reason of service, education, hospitality

[4] Shekleton, *Doctrinal Interpretation of Law*, The Catholic University of America Canon Law Studies, No. 345 (Washington, D. C.: The Catholic University of America Press, 1961), p. 52.

[5] Cicognani, *Canon Law* (Philadelphia: The Dolphin Press, 1934), p. 79. In view of the requirements for authentic interpretation, as outlined above, the term "official" employed by Cicognani must not be construed to mean "authentic."

[6] "[Curent superiores locales] ut saltem bis in mense, firmo praescripto can. 565, § 2, christianae catechesis habeatur instructio pro conversis et familiaribus, audientium conditioni accommodata, et, praesertim in religionibus laicalibus, pia ad omnes de familia exhortatio."

or ill health. [7] The other opinion understands "*familiares*" to mean domestic servants who dwell in the religious house. [8] The latter interpretation is the one adopted by the List of Questions. Question 86 reads:

> Do superiors see to it that, according to the Constitutions and common law, there be spiritual and catechetical instructions for the entire house (c. 509, § 2, 2°), for the novices (c. 565, § 2), for the scholastics (c. 588, § 1), for the *conversi*, for the domestics and servants (c. 509, § 2, 2°). [9]

While signifying that the Sacred Congregation understands "*familiares*" to mean "servants," Question 86 raises further questions of its own. It seems to indicate that canon 565, § 2, requires spiritual and catechetical instruction for *all* novices, whereas in fact the canon requires the instruction only for novices who are *conversi*. [10] The question likewise implies that *catechetical* instructions should be given to clerical students. But canon 588, § 1, does not specify that the instructions given to them be of a catechetical nature. [11] Canon 509 itself does not require that the pious exhortation delivered to the whole community be in the form of a catechetical instruction, [12] although Question 86 seems to imply this. Should it be concluded that Question 86 is also interpreting these canons along the lines indicated? No. For Question 86 itself includes the qualification, "according to the Constitutions and the common law." Therefore, while it can be held that the ques-

[7] Beste, *Introductio in Codicem*, p. 358; Coronata, *Institutiones Iuris Canonici*, I, 665, n. 540, Ramos, "De conditione Saecularium in Domibus Religiosorum,"— *CpR*, VI (1925), 140. Schaefer (*De Religiosis*, p. 268, n. 539) cites without disapproval authors who hold this opinion, though he does not hold it himself.

[8] Schaefer, *loc. cit.;* Vermeersch-Creusen, *Epitome*, I, p. 467, n. 629; Creusen-Ellis, *Religious Men and Women in Church Law*, pp. 69-70; Larraona, "Commentarium Codicis,"— *CpR*, VIII (1927), 172.

[9] The Latin version has "*familiaribus*" for the last word.

[10] Can. 565, § 2: "Conversi praeterea diligenter in christiana doctrina instituantur, speciali collatione ad eos habita semel saltem in hebdomada."

[11] Can. 588, § 1: "Toto studiorum curriculo religiosi committantur speciali curae Praefecti seu Magistri spiritus qui eorum animos ad vitam religiosam informet opportunis monitis, instructionibus atque exhortationibus."

[12] Cf. *supra*, p. 91, note 6.

tion interprets the controversial term "*familiares*," it does not seek to change the prescriptions of canons 565, 588 or 509. It is merely inquiring about their application to the various classes, as outlined and understood in the canons themselves.

ARTICLE II. "*Collegium*" IN CANON 544, § 3.

Canon 544, § 3, directs that testimonial letters be sought on behalf of those candidates who have been in a seminary, in a college, or in the postulancy or novitiate of another religious institute prior to their entrance into religious life.[13] There is a divergence of opinion among the authors over the meaning of "*collegium*" in this canon. One opinion holds that the term applies only to a school wherein training is given for the priestly or religious life.[14] Another holds that all boarding students in a school staffed by by religious or clerical personnel need testimonial letters to enter religious life.[15] This difference among the authors is settled in favor of the former opinion by Question 153, b), which reads:

> At least before entrance into the novitiate, were the following testimonial letters demanded and obtained:...
> b) The special testimonial letters which are to be given under oath by the Rector or Major Superior for those who have been in a Seminary or *a residence hall which is equivalent to an ecclesiastical one* [emphasis added], or in a postulantship or novitiate of a religious Institute (c. 544, § 3).

In view of the interpretation the question puts on the word "*collegium*" it can be concluded that the *college* in question is not a school for lay students.

13 "Si agatur de admittendis illis qui in Seminario, collegio vel alius religionis postulatu aut novitiatu fuerunt, requiruntur praeterea litterae testimoniales, datae pro diversis casibus a rectore Seminarii vel collegii, audito Ordinario loci, aut a maiore religionis Superiore,"

14 Beste, *Introductio in Codicem*, p. 390; Creusen-Ellis, *Religious Men and Women in Church Law*, p. 143; Coronata, *Institutiones Iuris Canonici*, I, 720, n. 574; Schaefer, *De Religiosis*, p. 454 n. 826.

15 Larraona, "Consultationes," *CpR*, I (1920), 180.

Article III. The Investment of a Dowry

Canon 549 directs that the dowry of a woman religious be invested following her first profession. The superioress charged with the investment is to seek the advice of her council and the consent of the local ordinary, as well as that of the regular superior if the house be dependent on him. [16] In general, the authors hold that the vote of the council is merely a consultative one unless the particular constitutions specify that it is a deliberative vote. [17] Biederlack (1845-1930) Führich (1869-1934) [18] and Blat (1870-1943) [19], however, maintained that the vote is a deliberative one. Vermeersch-Creusen strongly disagreed with this opinion, and considered that it could be abandoned. [20] Question 191, however, understands the vote as a deliberative one, when it asks:

> Were the dowries, immediately after the first profession, always invested by the Major Superioress, with the deliberative vote of her Council and the consent of the Ordinary of the place where the capital of the dowries is kept (c. 549).

Therefore, it can be concluded that the Sacred Congregation of Religious considers that the advice of the council required for the investment of the dowry constitutes a deliberative vote.

[16] "Post primam religiosae professionem dos in tutis, licitis ac fructiferis nominibus collocetur ab Antista cum suo Consilio, de consensu Ordinarii loci et Superioris regularis, si domus ab hoc dependeat..."

[17] Cf. Schaefer, *De Religiosis*, p. 472, n. 848; Beste, *Introductio in Codicem*, p. 394; Coronata, *Institutiones Iuris Canonici*, I, 727, n. 577; Vermeersch-Creusen, *Epitome*, I, 515, n. 699; Larraona, "Commentarium Codicis,"— *CpRM*, XXI (1940), 31-32; Kealy, *Dowry of Women Religious*, The Catholic University of America Canon Law Studies, No. 134 (Washington, D.C.: The Catholic University of America Press, 1941), pp. 89-90.

[18] *De Religiosis* (Oeniponte, 1919), n. 79—as cited by Vermeersch-Creusen, *loc. cit.*

[19] *Commentarium Textus Codicis Iuris Canonici*, Liber II, Partes II et III, *Ius de Religiosis et Laicis* (3. ed., Romae: Apud "Angelicum," 1938), 237, n. 244.

[20] *Epitome, loc.cit.*

ARTICLE IV. THE QUASI-DOWRY

By "quasi-dowry" is meant here the sum of money which a candidate for the religious life presents for her dowry, over and above the amount specified by the constitutions. The Code is silent about this contingency. Most of the authors agree, however, that unless it be forbidden by the constitutions, the candidate may, with the consent of the superioress, present as a dowry a sum larger than the amount specified. This sum is then to be handled on the same basis as the dowry, in regard to its investment, administration, transference and restoration.[21] Mayer[22] and Mothon[23] are in disagreement with this doctrine. They hold that an amount higher than the regulation dowry can neither be asked for nor received.

The *Elenchus Quaestionum* contains three questions pertinent to this point:

> 194. Is all property which is brought in as dowry, even though it be in excess of the sum required for a dowry in the constitutions, or even though there be in the Congregation no obligation to bring in a dowry, accepted, invested, administered, etc., with the observance of the norms which govern dowries.
>
> 195. In case of the departure of a professed religious, for whatever cause it occurred, and in case of transfer, were the dowry and likewise the personal belongings which the novice brought with her at her entrance, in the condition in which they were when she left, restored to the religious departing or transferring, without the income which had already accrued (cc. 551, 570, § 2).
>
> 196. Is this done also with property freely contributed for increasing the dowry even beyond the sum required by the constitutions.

21 Cf. Vermeersch-Creusen, *Epitome*, 514, n. 698; Schaefer, *De Religiosis*, p. 468, n. 843; Coronata, *Institutiones Iuris Canonici*, I, 724, n. 577; Kealy, *Dowry of Women Religious*, p. 70; Larraona, "Commentarium Codicis,"—*CpRM*, XX (1939), 11.

22 *Benediktinisches Ordensrecht in der Beuroner Kongregation* (4 vols., Beuron: Kuntsverlag, 1929-1936), III, 68.

23 *Traité sur l'État Religieux* (Paris: Societé Saint-Augustin, Desclée, De Brouwer, 1922), pp. 546-547, footnote 1.

From the wording of these questions it is evident which opinion has been adopted by the Sacred Congregation of Religious. Question 194 presupposes that a sum larger than that required by the constitutions may be accepted as a dowry. If accepted, this sum is to be administered with the observance of the norms which govern dowries. Question 196 implies that, in practice, the Sacred Congregation wishes that all of this sum be returned to the religious if she leaves the institute.

Article V. Absence from a Religious House

Canon 606, § 2, forbids superiors in the absence of a grave cause to give permission to be absent from a house of the institute; and if this absence is to extend beyond six months, the permission of the Holy See is necesssary, unless it be for the sake of studies.[24] Although the canon seems clear enough in giving the pursuit of studies as the only exception to the rule, some authors, following the lead of Vermeersch, have long taught that no permission of the Holy See is necessary for an absence beyond six months when this absence is necessitated by some work of the ministry proper to the religious institute.[25] Oesterle disagrees with this opinion. He holds that the permission of the Holy See is required, even if the absence is necessary for carrying out works proper to the institute.[26]

In practice this difference of opinion is settled by the interpretation afforded in Question 263:

[24] "Superioribus fas non est, salvis praescriptis can. 621-624, permittere ut subditi extra domum propriae religionis degant, nisi gravi et iusta de causa atque ad tempus quo fieri potest brevius secundum constitutiones; pro absentia vero quae sex menses excedat, nisi causa studiorum intercedat, semper Apostolicae Sedis venia requiritur."

[25] Cf. Vermeersch, "De Commoratione extra propriae religionis domum," — *Periodica de Re Canonica, Morali, Liturgica*, X (1922), (36)-(37); Coronata, *Institutiones Iuris Canonici*, I, p. 798, n. 612; Schaefer, *De Religiosis*, p. 707, n. 1191; De Carlo, *Jus Religiosorum* (Parisiis-Tornaci-Romae: Desclée et Socii, 1950), p. 300, n. 361.

[26] *Praelectiones Iuris Canonici*, I (Romae: In Collegio S. Anselmi, 1931), p. 340.

> For absences which exceed six months, except for studies or ministries according to the law and the Constitutions, was the permission of the Holy See always obtained (c. 606, § 2).

The mind of the Sacred Congregation of Religious in regard to this point is further illustrated by its Instruction on religious military chaplains. This instruction states:

> The religious military chaplain is... to be numbered... among those who... are legitimately absent to work in the sacred ministry, remaining subject to their superiors (canon 606, § 2).[27]

Superiors should use caution, however, in allowing their subjects to be absent for periods which exceed six months, even for the purpose of exercising a ministry proper to the institute. Although the opinion allowing such absences without an indult is defended by authors and is adopted in the List of Questions, there remains the necessity for each religious to observe community life. This is a necessity dictated both by the law[28] and by rules of prudence. An indiscriminate application of this opinion could, hypothetically, lead to the absurdity of sending all priests away from the community on the plea that any priestly work is proper to an approved clerical institute. Therefore superiors should judge prudently as to the necessity of each case and its compatiblity with the religious state and the particular nature of the institute. Superiors would also do well to establish prudent rules safeguarding the religious life of those subjects who are allowed to be absent for extended periods of time.[29]

[27] S. Cong. de Rel., instr. 2 febr. 1955, art. VI, 1: "Cappellanus militum religiosus non est cum exclaustratis (can. 639) eodem habendus numero, sed cum religiosis, qui sacri ministerii causa, suis obnoxii Moderatoribus, dum in officio tenentur, legitime absunt (can. 606, § 2)" — *AAS*, XLVII (1955), 95.

[28] Cf. can. 487, 594, 606, § 2.

[29] Cf. O'Brien, *The Provincial Religious Superior*, The Catholic University of America Canon Law Studies, No. 258 (Washington, D. C.: The Catholic University of America Press, 1947), p. 120.

CONCLUSIONS

1. Although the Holy See has always had the right to supervise religious institutes, it did not exercise this right extensively in the early centuries of the Church. (Cf. pp. 4-6.)

2. Following the IV Lateran Council (1215), the Holy See began to supervise religious in a detailed manner. Among the forms which this supervision assumed during this period were the following:

(a) new religious institutes were required to obtain papal approval (cf. pp. 12-16);

(b) the office of cardinal protector was introduced (cf. pp.16-17);

(c) supervisors of the cloister were appointed (cf. pp. 17-18);

(d) visitators were commissioned to act in the name of the Holy See (cf. pp. 18-21);

(e) there were instituted in the Roman Curia Congregations to supervise religious (cf. pp. 21-24);

(f) reports concerning religious were required from local ordinaries (cf. pp. 25-28);

(g) occasional reports were required from religious institutes (cf. pp. 29-31.)

3. In the nineteenth century the Holy See began to require periodic reports from newly approved religious institutes of pontifical approval. (Cf. p. 31-32.)

4. The first general law requiring such reports is to be found in canon 510. It provides that reports must be submitted every five years, unless the constitutions specify a shorter interval. Independent houses and institutes of diocesan approval were exempt from the obligation of submitting a report. (Cf. pp. 35-36.)

5. The decree *Sancitum est* (March 2, 1922) did not alter the provisions of canon 510, nor did it add new obligations substantially differing from those which are specified in the canon. (Cf. pp. 36-38.)

6. The decree *Cum transactis* (July 9, 1947) did add various obligations beyond the prescriptions of canon 510. (Cf. pp. 38-39, 40, 44.)

7. Superiors are not obliged to observe the prescriptions of the decree *Cum transactis* by virtue of the vow of obedience. Obligations arising from the decree which exceed the prescriptions of canon 510 have true binding force, not as laws, but as common jurisdictional precepts emanating from the legitimate administrative authority of the Sacred Congregation of Religious. (Cf. pp. 48-51.)

8. The efforts required to garner the information for the report provide religious superiors with a valuable opportunity for exercising necessary and useful supervision over their subjects. (Cf. pp. 77-78.)

9. The *Elenchus Quaestionum* forms a means of ascertaining the mind of the Holy See in regard to particular points of religious discipline in matters not covered by the Code of Canon Law. (Cf. pp. 57-76.)

10. In signing the reports of pontifically approved religious institutes of women, the primary function of the local ordinary is to authenticate the documents. However, he may use the occasion to acquire information about those matters which are committed to his supervision by canon 618. (Cf. pp. 83-85.)

11. The local ordinary is to add his comments to the reports of independent monasteries and houses, even though such monasteries or houses may pertain to male religious or to exempt religious. This fact is an indication that the Holy See wishes the local ordinary to be cognizant of the affairs of independent houses. However, his right and obligation to comment on the report does not give him more jurisdiction over these houses than that which is assigned to him by law. (Cf. pp. 88-89.)

12. The *Elenchus Quaestionum* serves as a source of doctrinal interpretation, when through it the Sacred Congregation of Religious adopts one or the other opinion in regard to certain disputed points. (Cf. pp. 90-97.)

BIBLIOGRAPHY

Sources

Acta Apostolicae Sedis, Commentarium Officiale, Romae: Typis Polyglottis Vaticanis, 1909-

Acta et Decreta Sacrorum Conciliorum Recentiorum, Collectio Lacensis, Auctoribus Presbyteris S. J. e domo B.V.M. sine Labe Conceptae ad Lacum, 7 vols., Friburgi Brisgoviae, 1870-1892.

Acta Sanctae Sedis, 41 vols., Romae, 1865-1908.

Bullarium Franciscanum Romanorum Pontificum, ed. Ioannes Sbaralea, Vol. I-IV, Romae, 1759-1768; ed. Conradus Eubel, Vol. V-VII, Romae, 1898-1904.

Bullarium Ordinis Fratrum Praedicatorum, opera Thomae Ripoll editum et ab Antonio Bremond illustratum, 8 vols., Romae, 1729-1740.

Bullarium Diplomatum et Privilegiorum Sanctorum Romanorum Pontificum Taurinensis Editio, 24 vols. et Appendix, Augustae Taurinorum et Neapoli, 1857-1872.

Canonical Legislation concerning Religious: Authorized English Translation, Westminster, Maryland: The Newman Press, 1948.

Canon Law Digest, The, Vols. I-IV and Supplements, 1917-1960, eds. T.L. Bouscaren-James J. O'Connor, Milwaukee: Bruce Publishing Co., 1934-1961.

Codex Iuris Canonici Pii X Pontificis Maximi iussu digestus Benedicti Papae XV auctoritate promulgatus, Romae, 1917.

Codicis Iuris Canonici Fontes, cura E.mi Petri Card. Gasparri editi, 9 vols., Romae (postea Civitate Vaticana): Typis Polyglottis Vaticanis, 1923-1939; Vols. VII-IX, ed. cura et studio E.mi Iustiniani Card. Serédi.

Collectanea in Usum Secretariae Sacrae Congregationis Episcoporum et Regularium, cura A. Bizzarri Archiepiscopi Philippensis Secretarii edita, 2. ed., Romae, 1885.

Constitutio Apostolica "Sedes Sapientiae" eique adnexa "Statuta Generalia," 2. ed., Romae: Apud Custodiam Librariam Sacrae Congregationis de Religiosis, 1957.

Corpus Iuris Canonici, editio Lipsiensis secunda post Aemilii Ludovici Richteri curas ad librorum manu scriptorum et editionis Romanae fidem recognovit et adnotatione critica instruxit Aemilius Friedberg, 2 vols., Lipsiae, 1879-1881.

Elenchus Quaestionum quibus a Religionibus et Societatibus in Relatione ad Sanctam Sedem quinto quoque anno transmittenda respondendum est ad normam Decreti "Cum transactis," Pro Religionibus et Societatibus Iuris Pontificii, Romae: Typis Polyglottis Vaticanis, 1949.

Elenchus Quaestionum quibus a Religionibus et Societatibus in Relatione ad Sanctam Sedem quinto quoque anno transmittenda respondendum est ad normam Decreti "Cum trans-

actis," Pro Monasteriis et Domibus Religiosis Sui Iuris non Foederatis, Romae: Typis Polyglottis Vaticanis, 1957.

Elenchus Quaestionum quibus a Religionibus et Societatibus in Relatione ad Sanctam Sedem quinto quoque anno transmittenda respondendum est ad normam Decreti "Cum transactis," Pro Congregationibus et Societatibus Iuris Dioecesani, Romae: Typis Polyglottis Vaticanis, 1957.

Jaffé, Philippus, *Regesta Pontificum Romanorum ab condita Ecclesia ad annum post Christum natum MCXCVIII,* 2. ed., correctam et auctam auspiciis Gulielmi Wattenbach, curaverunt S. Loewenfeld, F. Kaltenbrunner, P. Ewald, 2 vols. in 1, Lipsiae, 1885-1888.

List of Questions Which are to be Answered by Religious Institutes and Societies in the Report to be Sent to the Holy See every Five Years according to the Decree "Cum transactis," The, For Religious Institutes and Societies of Pontifical Right, Rome: Polyglot Printing Press, 1957.

Mansi, Joannes D., *Sacrorum Conciliorum Nova et Amplissima Collectio,* 53 vols. in 59, Parisiis, Arnhem, Lipsiae, 1901-1927.

Normae Secundum quas S. Congr. Episcoporum et Regularium Procedere Solet in Approbandis Novis Institutis Votorum Simplicium, Romae, 1901.

Regula et Constitutiones Generales Fratrum Minorum, Ad Claras Aquas (Quaracchi), 1922.

Regula et Constitutiones Generales Ordinis Fratrum Minorum, Romae: Curia Generalis Ordinis, 1953.

Rituale Romano-Seraphicum Ordinis Fratrum Minorum, 3. ed., Romae: Schola Typographica "Pax et Bonum", 1955.

Schroeder, Henry, *Canons and Decrees of the Council of Trent,* Original text with English translation, St. Louis: B. Herder Book Co., 1941.

Schwartz, Eduardus, *Acta Conciliorum Oecumenicorum (a concilio Ephesino a. 431 ad conc. Constantinopolitanum a. 879)* 11 vols. in 4°, Tom. II, *Concilium Universale Chalcedonense,* Vol. 2, pars 2, *Rerum Chalcedonensium Collectio Vaticana, Canones et Symbolum,* Berolini et Lipsiae: Walter de Gruyter et Co., 1936.

Sylloge Praecipuorum Documentorum Recentium Summorum Pontificum et S. Congregationis de Propaganda Fide necnon Aliarum SS. Congregationum Romanarum ad usum Missionariorum, Romae: Typis Polyglottis Vaticanis, 1939.

Reference Works

Barraclough, Geoffrey, *Mediaeval Germany, 911-1250: Essays by German Historians,* 2 vols., Oxford: Basil Blackwell, Ltd., 1938.

Bastien, Pierre, *Directoire Canonique à l'Usage des Congregations à Vœux Simples,* Abbaye de Maredsous, 1904.

Bernardino da Siena, *Il Cardinale Protettore negli Istituti Religiosi specialmente negli Ordini Francescani,* Dissertatio ad Lauream in Facultate Iuris Canonici Pontificiae Universitatis Gregorianae, Firenze: Industria Tipografica Fiorentina, 1940.

Benedictus XIV, *De Synodo Dioecesana*, 2 vols., Parmae, 1764.

Beste, Udalricus, *Introductio in Codicem*, 4. ed., Neapoli: M. D'Auria, 1956.

Blat, Albertus, *Commentarium Textus Codicis Iuris Canonici*, Liber II, Partes II et III, *Ius de Religiosis et Laicis*, 3. ed., Romae Apud "Angelicum," 1938.

Bouix, Dominicus, *De Curia Romana*, 2. ed., Parisiis, 1880.

———. *Tractatus de Jure Regularium*, 3. ed., 2 vols., Parisiis, 1882-1883.

Bouscaren, T. Lincoln — Ellis, Adam, *Canon Law, A Text and Commentary*, third revised edition, Milwaukee: The Bruce Publishing Company, 1958.

Brockhaus, Thomas Aquinas, *Religious Who Are Known as "Conversi,"* The Catholic University of America Canon Law Studies, No. 225, Washington, D.C.: The Catholic University of America Press, 1946.

Catholic Encyclopedia, The, 15 vols., New York, 1907-1912; Index vol., 1914; Supplement, 1922.

Chelodi, Joannes, *Ius de Personis iuxta Codicem Iuris Canonici, Praemisso Tractatu de Principiis et Fontibus Iuris Canonici*, ed. altera, a Sac. Ernesto Bertagnolli recognita et aucta, Tridenti: Libr. Edit. Tridentum, 1927.

Cicognani, Amleto, *Canon Law*, authorized English translation, Philadelphia: The Dolphin Press, 1934.

Coronata, Mattheus Conte a, *Institutiones Iuris Canonici*, 2. ed., 5 vols., Taurini: Marietti, 1939-1947.

Creusen, Iosephus, *De Iuridica Status Religiosi Evolutione*, 2. ed., Romae: Apud Aedes Pontificiae Universitatis Gregorianae, 1948.

Creusen, Joseph-Ellis, Adam, *Religious Men and Women in Church Law*, 6. English Ed., Milwaukee: Bruce Publishing Company, 1958.

De Carlo, Camillus, *Jus Religiosorum*, Parisiis-Tornaci-Romae: Desclée et Socii, 1950.

Dudden, F. Homes, *Gregory the Great*, 2 vols., London, 1905.

Fagnanus, Prosper, *Commentaria in Quinque Libros Decretalium*, 4 vols., Venetiis, 1697.

Fanfani, Louis-O'Rourke, Kevin, *Canon Law for Religious Women*, Dubuque, Iowa: The Priory Press, 1961.

Farrell, Benjamin, *The Rights and Duties of the Local Ordinary regarding Congregations of Women Religious of Pontifical Approval*, The Catholic University of America Canon Law Studies, No. 128, Washington, D.C.: The Catholic University of America Press, 1941.

Ferraris, F. Lucius, *Bibliotheca Canonica, Iuridica, Moralis, Theologica, necnon Ascetica, Polemica, Rubristica, Historica*, 9 vols., Romae, 1885-1899.

Fogliasso, Aemilius, *De Extensione Iuridica Instituti Exemptionis Religiosorum*, Romae: Apud Custodiam Librariam Pont. Instituti Utriusque Iuris, 1948.

Freriks, Celestine, *Religious Congregations in their External Relations*, The Catholic University of America Canon Law Studies, No. 1, Washington, D.C., 1916.

Holzapfel, Heribertus, *Manuale Historiae Ordinis Fratrum Minorum*, latine redditum a Gallo Haselbeck, Friburgi Brisgoviae, 1909.

Kealy, Thomas, *Dowry of Women Religious,* The Catholic University of America Canon Law Studies, No. 134, Washington, D.C.: The Catholic University of America Press, 1941.

Knowles, David, *The Monastic Order In England,* Cambridge: The University Press, 1941.

Kurtscheid, Bertrandus, *Historia Iuris Canonici,* 2 vols., Vol. I, *Historia Institutorum,* Romae: Officium Libri Catholici, 1941.

Larraona, Arcadio, ed altri collaboratori, *La Nuova Disciplina Canonica sulle Monache,* Romae: Desclée e C., 1952.

Lucidi, Angelus, *De Visitatione Sacrorum Liminum,* 3. ed., 3 vols., ed. J. Schneider, Romae, 1883.

Lynch, Timothy, *Contracts between Bishops and Religious Congregations,* The Catholic University of America Canon Law Studies, No. 239, Washington, D.C.: The Catholic University of America Press, 1946.

Mayer, Heinrich, *Benediktinisches Ordensrecht in der Beuroner Kongregation,* 4 vols., Beuron: Kuntsverlag, 1929-1936.

Michiels, Gommarus, *Normae Generales Juris Canonici,* 2. ed., 2 vols., Parisiis-Tornaci-Romae: Desclée et Socii, 1949.

Migne, J.P., *Patrologiae Corpus Completum, Series Graeca,* 161 vols., Parisiis, 1857-1866.

———, *Patrologiae Corpus Completum, Series Latina,* 221 vols., 1844-1855.

Monin, Arthur, *De Curia Romana,* Lovanii, 1912.

Mothon, Joseph, *Traité sur l'État Religieux,* Paris: Societé Saint-Augustin, Desclée, De Brouwer, 1922.

Muzzarelli, Fridericus, *De Congregationibus Iuris Dioecesani,* Romae: Apud Piam Societatem a S. Paulo Apostolo, 1943.

O'Brien, Romaeus, *The Provincial Religious Superior,* The Catholic University of America Canon Law Studies, No. 258, Washington, D.C.: The Catholic University of America Press, 1947.

Oesterle, Gerardus, *Praelectiones in Codicem Iuris Canonici,* Vol. I, Romae: Apud Collegium S. Anselmi, 1931.

Orth, Clement, *The Approbation of Religious Institutes,* The Catholic University of America Canon Law Studies, No. 71, Washington, D.C.: The Catholic University of America, 1931.

Quinn, Stephen, *Relation of the Local Ordinary to Religious of Diocesan Approval,* The Catholic University of America Canon Law Studies, No. 283, Washington, D.C.: The Catholic University of America Press, 1949.

Reilly, Thomas, *The Visitation of Religious,* The Catholic University of America Canon Law Studies, No. 112, Washington, D.C.: The Catholic University of America, 1938.

Roelker, Edward, *Precepts,* Paterson, New Jersey: St. Anthony Guild Press, 1955.

Schaaf, Valentine, *The Cloister,* The Catholic University of America Canon Law Studies, No. 13, Cincinnati, Ohio, 1921.

Schaefer, Timotheus, *De Religiosis*, 4. ed., Romae: Editrice "Apostolato Cattolico," 1947.

Schmidt, John Rogg, *The Principles of Authentic Interpretation in Canon 17 of the Code of Canon Law*, The Catholic University of America Canon Law Studies, No. 141, Washington, D.C.: The Catholic University of America Press, 1941.

Schroeder, Henry, *Disciplinary Decrees of the General Councils*, Text, translation and commentary, St. Louis, Mo.: B. Herder Co., 1937.

Sheehy, Robert, *The Sacred Congregation of the Sacraments*, The Catholic University of America Canon Law Studies, No. 333, Washington, D.C.: The Catholic University of America Press, 1954.

Shekleton, Matthew, *Doctrinal Interpretation of Law*, The Catholic University of America Canon Law Studies, No. 345, Washington, D.C.: The Catholic University of America Press, 1961.

Toso, A., *Ad Codicem Iuris Canonici Commentaria Minora*, 5 vols., Romae: Marietti, 1920-1927.

Van Espen, Zegerus Bernardus, *Ius Ecclesiasticum Universum*, 2. ed., 4 vols., Lovanii et Lugduni, 1778.

Van Hove, A., *Commentarium Lovaniense in Codicem Iuris Canonici*, Vol. I, Tom. II, *De Legibus Ecclesiasticis*, Mechliniae-Romae: H. Dessain, 1930.

Vermeersch, A.-Creusen, J., *Epitome Iuris Canonici*, 7. ed., 3 vols., Mechliniae-Romae: H. Dessain, 1949-1956.

Wernz, Franciscus X., *Ius Decretalium ad Usum Praelectionum in Scholis Textus Iuris Canonici, sive Iuris Decretalium*, 6 vols., Vol. III, pars 2, 2. ed., Romae, 1908.

Articles

Almond, J.C., "Oblati, Oblatae, Oblates," *The Catholic Encyclopedia*, XI, 188-189.

Coogan, John, "Do We Need Direction?" *Review for Religious*, I (1942), 376-381.

Ellis, Adam C., "First Annual Report," *Review for Religious*, IX (1950), 309-316.

———, "Quinquennial Report, 1951," *Review for Religious*, X (1951), 20-24.

Frison, Basilius, "Adnotationes," *CpRM*, XXXVII (1958), 274-282.

———, "The Laws of Training in the Apostolic Constitution, *Sedes Sapientiae*," *The Jurist*, XXI (1961), 204-235; 375-397.

Gallen, Joseph F., "The Quinquennial Report: Obligations and Directives," *Review for Religious*, XI (1952), 12-18; 69-74.

Gutiérrez, A., "Della Relazione Quinquennale da Farsi alla Santa Sede," *La Nuova Disciplina Canonica sulle Monache*, Arcadio Larraona ed altri collaboratori, Roma: Desclée e C., 1952, pp. 232-260.

———, "Introductio in Constitutionem Apostolicam 'Sedes Sapientiae'," *CpRM*, XXXVI (1957), 127-141; 227-234; 316-327; XXXVII (1958), 35-45.

Hirsch, Hans, "The Constitutional History of the Reformed Monasteries during the Investiture Contest," *Mediaeval Germany, 911-1250: Essays by German Historians*, tr. Barraclough, 2 vols., Oxford: Basil Blackwell, Ltd., 1938, II, 133-173.

Huot, M., "Adnotationes," *Monitor Ecclesiasticus*, LXXXIII (1958), 241-247.

Larraona, Arcadius, "Commentarium Codicis," *CpR*, I (1920), 16-21, 45-50, 133-140, 171-177, 209-217, 345-349; *CpR*, VI (1925), 79-83, 127-135; *CpR*, VIII (1927), 164-176, 275-283; *CpRM*, XX (1939), 8-17; *CpRM*, XXI (1940), 26-35.

———, "Consultationes," *CpR*, I (1920), 179-183.

Pugliese, Augustinus, "Adnotationes de Quinquennali Relatione a Religionibus, a Societatibus Vitae Communis et ab Institutis Saecularibus Facienda," *Monitor Ecclesiasticus*, LXXV (1950), 188-198.

Ramos, Domitius, "De Conditione Saecularium in Domibus Religiosorum," *CpR*, VI (1925), 136-140.

"Spiritual Direction by the Ordinary Confessor" (editorial), *Review for Religious*, I (1942), 218-222.

Stutz, Ulrich, "The Proprietary Church as a Element of Mediaeval Germanic Ecclesiastical Law," *Mediaeval Germany, 911-1250: Essays by German Historians*, tr. Barraclough, 2 vols., Oxford: Basil Blackwell, Ltd., II, 35-70.

Tabera, A., "De Ordinatione Status Monachalis in Fontibus Iustinianeis," *CpR*, XIV (1933), 86-95, 199-206; XV (1934), 412-418.

"The List of Questions Which are to be Answered by Religious Institutes and Societies in the Report to be Sent to the Holy See every Five Years according to the Decree *Cum transactis*," *Review for Religious*, IX (1950), 52-56, 108-112, 166-168, 209-224, 269-278.

Vermeersch, A., "De Commoratione extra propriae religionis domum." *Periodica de Re Canonica, Morali, Liturgica*, X (1922), (36)-(37).

———, "Religious Life," *The Catholic Encyclopedia*, XII, 748-762.

Periodicals

Analecta Iuris Pontificii, Romae, 1855-1868; Parisiis, 1869-1891.

Commentarium pro Religiosis, Romae, 1920- ; ab anno 1935: *Commentarium pro Religiosis et Missionariis*.

Jurist, The, Washington, D.C., 1941-

Monitor Ecclesiasticus, Romae, 1948- (annis 1876-1948, *Il Monitore Ecclesiastico*).

Periodica de Religiosis et Missionariis, Brugis. 1905-1919; ab anno 1920: *Periodica de Re Canonica et Morali utilia praesertim Religiosis et Missionariis*, Brugis, 1920-1927; *Periodica de Re Morali, Canonica, Liturgica*, Brugis, 1927-1936, et Romae, 1937-

Review for Religious, St. Marys, Kansas, 1942-

ABBREVIATIONS

AAS— *Acta Apostolicae Sedis.*

Bull. Fran. — *Bullarium Franciscanum Romanorum Pontificum Taurinensis Editio.*

CLD— *Canon Law Digest.*

Collectanea— *Collectanea in Usum Secretariae Sacrae Congregationis Episcoporum et Regularium*, cura Bizzarri edita.

CpR— *Commentarium pro Religiosis.*

CpRM— *Commentarium pro Religiosis et Missionariis.*

Epitome— Vermeersch-Creusen, *Epitome Iuris Canonici.*

Fontes— *Codicis Iuris Canonici Fontes cura... Gasparri editi.*

Jaffé— *Regesta Pontificum Romanorum.*

Mansi— *Sacrorum Conciliorum Nova et Amplissima Collectio.*

MPL—Migne, *Patrologiae Cursus Completus, Series Latina.*

Normae— *Normae Secundum quas S. Congr. Episcoporum et Regularium Procedere Solet in Approbandis Novis Institutis Votorum Simplicium.*

ALPHABETICAL INDEX

BIOGRAPHICAL NOTE

Mel Lawrence Brady was born on May 9, 1922, in Detroit, Michigan. He received his primary education in Gesu parochial school, Detroit, and attended the University of Detroit High School for two years. He completed his high school studies at St. Francis Preparatory Seminary in Cincinnati, Ohio. On August 15, 1941, he entered the novitiate of the Cincinnati Province of the Order of Friars Minor. He made his profession of simple vows in the Order of Friars Minor on August 16, 1942. Three years later he made his solemn profession at Duns Scotus College, Detroit, Michigan. There he completed his philosophical studies, receiving the Bachelor of Arts degree in June, 1946. Thence he was sent to Holy Family Monastery, Oldenburg, Indiana, to pursue the prescribed theological studies. He was there ordained to the priesthood on June 8, 1950. In the autumn of that year, his superiors sent him to the School of Canon Law at the Catholic University of America, where he received the degree of the Licentiate in Canon Law in June, 1952. He continued his studies in Canon Law at the same University in the year 1961-1962.

CANON LAW STUDIES*

421. Quinn, Rev. Edmund, O.F.M.Cap., B.A., J.C.L., Archconfraternities, a sodalities and primary unions, with a supplement on the Archconfrater of Christian Mothers.
422. Brady, Rev. Mel Lawrence, O.F.M., B.A., J.C.L., The quinquennial re of religious institutes to the Holy See.
423. Brenkle, Rev. John J., B.A., J.C.L., The impediment of male impotence, w special application to paraplegia.
424. Christensen, Rev. Joseph Edward, J.C.L., Character requisites for recept of holy orders. (microfilm)
425. Paul, Rev. John J., M.S.C., S.T.L., J.C.L., The recipient of the sacrament penance. (microfilm)
426. Pavloff, Rev. George G., A.B., J.C.L., Papal judge delegates at the time the *Corpus Iuris Canonici.*
427. Reissner, Rev. Edward A., A.B., J.C.L. Canonical employer-employee r tionship: Canon 1524.
428. Schierse, Rev. Paul J., A.B., J.C.L., Laws of the State of Delaware affect church property.
429. Seasoltz, Rev. Robert Kevin, O.S.B., A.B., S.T.L., Directives on sacred and the building of a church. (microfilm)

*For a complete list of the available numbers of this series apply to Catholic University of America Press, 620 Michigan Avenue, N.E., Washington D.C., for a general catalogue.

www.ingramcontent.com/pod-product-compliance
Lightning Source LLC
LaVergne TN
LVHW050205080826
844660LV00012B/358

* 9 7 8 0 8 1 3 2 2 6 7 1 2 *